father Boyd

FATHER GOD, the Devil, and You

Father God, the Devil, and You
by father Boyd
Copyright © 2022

All rights reserved. No part of this publication may be reproduced, stored in a retrieval system, or transmitted in any form or by any means—for example, electronic, photocopy, and recording—without the prior written permission of the publisher. The only exception is brief quotations in printed reviews.

Cover Design and Editorial Work
Linda Stubblefield, Arrow Computer Services

Scripture questions my be directed to the following email address:
bberends1238@gmail.com

Dedication

This book is dedicated to our late son Todd. I started the book, *Father God, the Devil, and You*, some two years ago.

Shortly after beginning the research, the Devil took our son in death. From that time on to this day, the Devil has attacked our family relentlessly.

Every morning and evening I have found it necessary to ask Father God to place a hedge of protection around Linda and me. I asked Father God to wrap a protective covering around our heads, place the helmet of salvation over that, and ask Jesus to wrap the protection altogether.

Father God, and Jesus have done that faithfully. The few times that the protection was not adequate, I do not believe God was at fault, but something I was lacking in my prayer for protection. Each time I confessed to Father God my inadequate prayer, He reversed my oversight, and the Enemy was sent packing.

There is no question in my mind that there is a battle in the unseen realm that will continue until God pulls the plug for the last time.

The battle is ongoing between God and the Devil, but the more I have become personally engaged, the more I enjoy taking on the Devil, and watching the power in the name of Jesus defeat the Devil every time. My God is faithful.

– father Boyd

About the Author

MANY YEARS AGO when our children were teenagers, an Irish evangelist friend called the house one night. Our youngest daughter answered the phone, only to hear my Irish friend ask in his delightful Irish brogue, "Is 'Brother' Boyd home?"

Quick as a whip, she answered, **"No, Brother Boyd is not home, but father Boyd is. Would you like to talk to him?"**

When I began writing, I adopted that nomenclature as the author's name. As a father of five now well up in years and biblically a priest, I am three-fold qualified to use the title of "father."

This book has been written after many years of personal healings that made it obvious to me that Jesus is the Author and Provider of our healing, as well as our health.

The author's first book entitled, *God's Health Care Plan,* covered many years where Jesus proved to me that He is not only my Redeemer but also my Healer.

I have enjoyed over 60 years of trusting Jesus to heal me. **These years of trusting Him for healing have only deepened my faith in His promise for eternal life.**

Just as the Holy Spirit has led and directed me all these years in the healing ministry of Jesus in my life, *I have now been exposed to a deeper understanding of Father God and Satan, His enemy.*

I trust that this book will open in your heart a desire to know God in a deeper way and to increase your trust in Jesus to fulfill His promise of eternal life and living for eternity in heaven with Him.

Table of Contents

Introduction 9

Part One: Satan's Origin and History 13
   1:1 The Origin of Satan 14
   1:2 Satan's Creation 15
   1:3 God's Divine Council 18
   1:4 Satan's Rebellion 21
   1:5 Biblical Names of Satan 23
   1:6 Satan's Revolt Against God Spreads 25
   1:7 God's Destruction of His Wonderful Creation 28
   1:8 Meanwhile, What Was Happening in Heaven? 29

Part Two: Your Authority Over the Enemy 33
   2:9   God, and God Alone, Is Supreme 34
   2:10 What Is Authority? 37
   2:11 What Is the Christian's Authority? 40
   2:12 Your God-Given Authority Over Satan 41
   2:13 Your Authority Is a Delegated Authority 44
   2:14 Your Authority Is Now 46
   2:15 Each Encounter and for Every Time 47
   2:16 Jesus No Longer Deals Directly with the Devil 51
   2:17 Does Your God-Given Authority Extend to Others? ... 55
   2:18 What Part Does Faith Play in Your Authority? 56
   2:19 Learn to Be Exalted 59
   2:20 The Keys of Authority 60

Part Three: The Christian's Spiritual Warfare 63
   3:21 Your Authority Reviewed 65
   3:22 Jesus Went to Heaven as Head of the Church 66
   3:23 Your Authority Is Now 70
   3:24 Reigning as Kings 71
   3:25 Temptation: From Where Does It Come? 73
   3:26 Free Will Always Prevails 77
   3:27 It Always Comes Down to Your Choice 79
   3:28 Satanic Oppression or Possession? 79
   3:29 Christians Can Only Be Oppressed 80
   3:30 Satan and His Followers Are Active Everywhere 84
   3:31 Satanic Preparation, Now and for Eternity 85
   3:32 In It to Win It 87
   3:33 Most of Today's Christians Deny that Power 88

Part Four: Your Victory Over Satan Begins NOW 95
   4:34 Your Authority Review 96
   4:35 Remembering Where You Are 97
   4:36 Faith Review 98
   4:37 Who Are You Fighting? 99
   4:38 What Is a Spiritual Stronghold? 101
   4:39 Which God/god Would You Choose? 105
   4:40 Repentance Is Not an Emotion 107
   4:41 Satan's Boundaries 108
   4:42 Demonic Affiliations 110
   4:43 Demonic Spirits 112
   4:44 Strongholds Caused by Negative Emotions 116

Part Five: Conclusion, Summary, and Challenge 119

Introduction

Over the past 60 years, I have been on a pilgrimage. Jesus has been teaching me about the healing and health that He has restored to me. Jesus has also increased my biblical knowledge of healing, and He has increased the number of my personal healings.

For me to be healed also meant that I would have to experience more sickness, more disease, and more troubles. Just as more of these negative happenings came into my life, Jesus also increased the times that He healed me in every way.

Isaiah prophesied that Jesus would be lashed with stripes for our healing. Other prophets added that Jesus would not only be beaten with 39 lashes, He would also be humiliated, and His beard would be plucked out, **so that we could have healing restored.**

The number and intensity of my sicknesses and healings have been increased over these 60-plus years. **Healing has included the physical, the mental, and the emotional areas.** According to the World Health Organization, *healing* is "a state of complete physical, mental, and social well-being and not merely the absence of disease or infirmity."

Many times in recent years, the length of time between my prayers and healings have lengthened, and I could not figure out why.

Over a period of time, **God revealed the problem. He showed me that He had not changed and the stripes that Jesus bore at Calvary for my healing were still valid.**

What the Holy Spirit was teaching me is that my faith for healing had now *matured*; I had yet more to learn.

Then the Holy Spirit began to introduce me to the workings of God's enemy, the Devil. As I began to understand how the Devil hindered my healings, I was led by the Holy Spirit to learn more. **The more I learned, the more I learned that I needed to learn much more.**

For two years I have been asking the Holy Spirit to teach me more. Along the way Jesus made it clear that I needed to share the knowledge He had been teaching me.

The results of the leading and direction by the Holy Spirit and the power of Jesus Himself can be found in this book entitled *Father God, the Devil, and You.* **I never begin a day of research, a time of collating that research material, and finally a day of writing, until I ask the Holy Spirit not to let my eyes miss anything, my mind to understand what I have read, my memory to remember what I have read, and that the Holy Spirit not to let me miss anything He wants said.**

All the prophecies found in the Old Testament did indeed come to pass. **Jesus was crucified and died for our sins,** *which is all He had to do to save us from our sins!*

However, Jesus went even further. He allowed Himself to be whipped and humiliated. And His beard was plucked out so that we might have the gift of healing and health restored.

Jesus' resurrection resulted in Satan's being cast out of heaven. Jesus' victory over Satan made things both better and worse for those of His kids still here on earth.

Jesus' death for your sins is a gift Father God had planned from the day that Adam sinned, and mankind came under Satan's dominion. The gifts Jesus made possible through His suffering, death, and resurrection are yours—but only if you are willing to accept them.

*Jesus' victory over Satan is yours to enjoy through Him—***but only if you are willing by faith to believe the authority to do so is yours.**

Introduction

Healing and health are additional gifts that Jesus made available to the saints at Calvary, *but they are not automatic.* They do not come automatically with the gift of redemption.

Just as you accepted the death of Jesus to cancel your sins and provide an eternal life in heaven, you must accept by faith that Jesus suffered the beatings and the humiliation that He bore at Calvary.

I accepted this additional gift Jesus made possible in my life over 60 years ago. Since then, *in both theology and in actual healings,* I have been growing in knowledge, and I have been in receipt of the healing gifts personally, *as well as for my family.*

Only in these later years of experiencing the gifts of healing in my life has Jesus begun teaching me about the ways that Satan has hindered and delayed the healings Jesus has had for me when I needed them.

Sometimes Satan has delayed my healing, and sometimes Satan has made my sickness worse. During these times of delayed healing, I began to learn why and who was causing the delay.

When sickness or disease have occurred in my life *(and that has been often and sometimes very severe)* and my healing from Jesus has been delayed, I have had to ask Jesus why.

Sometimes something was in my life that should not have been there, and I had to repent of that and ask forgiveness. However, my sin was not always the case as Jesus began to teach me. Jesus showed me that many times the problem where my sickness had only gotten worse or my healing had not been forthcoming, *the problem was a spiritual problem, namely satanic or his demonic forces.*

This relatively newly learned knowledge inspired this book titled *Father God, the Devil, and You.* What began as a simple prayer request to Jesus as to what was happening in my healing has turned into something so much more.

The result of two years of experiences, learning and guidance by the Father, Son, and Holy Spirit has taught me many new and misunderstood spiritual matters involving God, the Devil and myself.

Over the past two years the Devil has attacked myself, my wife, and my family to hinder the writing of this book. I have learned much, experienced much, and now my prayer is that this book, which is the result of my prayers, my experiences, and my Holy Spirit guidance, will be a blessing to you in your fight against God's Enemy.

I can only trust that the Holy Spirit will use the words in this book to begin and/or strengthen you toward your healings and in the knowledge of your authority over the workings of Satan and his evil domain.

There is no question in my mind that not only is God Supreme, but God is also very good!

– father Boyd

PART ONE

Father God, the Devil, and You

Satan's Origin and History

Satan's Origin and History

Theologians have long debated the origin of Satan and where he fits into the overall scheme of things. There are as many theories as there are theologians. For the sake of this book, we will let *the* Book, the Bible, make the definition for us.

The apostle Paul in his letter to the Colossians wrote that Jesus Christ was created in the exact likeness of the unseen God. Other Scripture passages indicate that Jesus was *begotten*, which means "procreated or fathered." How Jesus came into being from the Father is not known. And Christ Himself made everything in heaven above and in the earth beneath.

Part 1:1
The Origin of Satan

The TLB translation of the following Colossians passage is very understandable, especially for those of us who are not theologians, biblically savvy pastors, or even biblical experts. Having presented the rationale for using this particular translation, the text reads as follows:

> "Christ is the exact likeness of the unseen God. He [Jesus] existed before God made anything at all, and in fact, ¹⁶Christ himself is the Creator who made everything in heaven and earth, the things we can see and the things we can't; the spirit world with its kings and kingdoms, its rulers and authorities; all were made

by Christ for his own use and glory. ¹⁷He [Christ] was before all else began and it is his power that holds everything together" (Colossians 1:15-17 TLB).

If you, the reader, are willing to accept this Bible translation in its entirety, then we will agree that God created Jesus Christ in His image with all that this passage implies. **And then Christ carried out what God desired by creating the angels first.**

Do we know all the details? No, we do not; but if you can agree with Paul, then it was Jesus, at God's direction and with His authority that the angels, including Lucifer, were created.

We do not know if Satan was created first or if the other angels were created before Satan. As to Who decided on the positions for the angelic heavenly realm, we can only presume it had to be God Himself.

We do know some of the details for the created angel known as Satan from Ezekiel 28. The theological experts agree the reference to the king of Tyre is really a reference to Satan, i.e., Lucifer.

Part 1:2
Satan's Creation

Once again, I would like to use the TLB translation from Ezekiel 28:12b–19 for purposes of understanding. (The reader can also reference other translations for comparison.) The Lord says,

"You were the perfection of wisdom and beauty. ¹³You were in Eden, the garden of God; your clothing was bejeweled with every precious stone—ruby, topaz, diamonds, chrysolite, onyx, jasper, sapphire, carbuncle, and emerald—all in beautiful settings of finest gold. They were given you on the day you were created. ¹⁴I

[God] *appointed you to be the anointed Guardian Angel. You had access to the holy mountain of God. You walked among the stones of fire.*

¹⁵You were perfect in all you did from the day you were created, until that time when wrong was found in you. ¹⁶Your great wealth filled you with inner turmoil, and you sinned. Therefore I cast you out of the mountain of God like a common sinner. I destroyed you, O Guardian Angel, from the midst of the stones of fire. ¹⁷Your heart was filled with pride because of all your beauty; you corrupted your wisdom for the sake of splendor. Therefore, I have cast you down to the ground and exposed you helpless before the gaze of kings. [Christians are considered kings in the Bible.] *¹⁸You defiled your holiness with lust for gain; therefore, I brought forth fire from your own actions and let it burn you to ashes upon the earth in sight of all those watching you. ¹⁹All who know you are appalled at your fate; you are an example of horror; you are destroyed forever."*

I would like to unpack this interesting and enlightening passage found in book of Ezekiel, which was written by the prophet Ezekiel many years after Satan was created. This passage containing Satan's sin information came straight from God. And making that statement when the passage starts with that observation helps in the understanding of this narrative.

When was Satan was created? Did he precede the other angels in creation? We are simply not told. We do know that no other angel is ever recorded as being created in a like manner of beauty.

I don't know all that *"perfection of wisdom and beauty"* really means, but I believe it is safe to say that Satan had no rivals in the angelic realm. God wanted no misunderstanding among the other angels, so God clothed Satan like no other—with jewels in excess and beauty set in the purest of gold.

God also gave Satan a position that would indicate he was above all the other angels. I will address more about the **Council of God** that met on the **Holy Mountain** later, but his was a very high and important position.

When you read the books of Isaiah, Ezekiel, Jeremiah, or Daniel, you are introduced to *"the stones of fire"* that surround the throne of God. That reference alone would be an indication that Satan's position was a high one that gave him direct access to God.

When you read the Bible in its entirety, Satan was probably the perfect angel until God decided to create humanity. Even that decision was likely acceptable with Satan at the time God suggested the idea. But when God said that His proposed new creation would be lower than the angels, but only for a time, *Satan's pride could not handle that thought. The idea of rebellion entered his mind and took root.*

Satan fulfilled his position perfectly until he let the **sin of pride** corrupt his thinking. What corrupted Satan was the same sin that corrupts us today. Pride was the very sin that corrupted Satan, and today, that same sin of pride continues to corrupt humans—*believers and unbelievers alike.*

In the Catholic religion, the sin of pride is considered the greatest of the seven deadliest sins. God made the decision to cast out Satan, accompanied by all the disgraces listed. **In God's mind, when He decrees something, it is as good as done**—*even though it may be many years in human time before His decree actually takes place.*

When God makes a "statement of determination," in His eyes it is as if it were already a done deal. So, all of this did not take place immediately because it was not until Jesus was resurrected and ascended to heaven was Satan cast out along with the other fallen angels.

Throughout the Bible are instances of Satan's still being in heaven. In the book of Job, Satan appears to still have his position on the council of God. Jesus in Matthew and John in Revelation make it clear that at the time they were speaking (or writing), Satan was still in heaven. It seems logical to assume that in God's eyes Satan's removal from heaven is considered done, but in the human time frame, these things God sees as done really evolve or happen over a period of time.

In summary, Jesus was involved in the creation of Satan, an angel who was created for a very high-ranking position and possibly even the highest rank in the angelic world.

Part 1:3
God's Divine Council

Clearly, God is a God of three parts: Father God, His Son Jesus, and His Holy Spirit. These are the only supreme beings in charge in heaven, and they are now and forever will be in charge. They are the supreme beings with whom we will spend eternity.

When God is mentioned in this book, that reference to God includes all three parts of God Himself.

Throughout the Bible references to a council of God can be found. God had elected to establish a council to oversee the carrying out of His wishes.

The first council consisted of Himself, Jesus, and the Holy Spirit. That council was later expanded to include certain angels, including Satan. For more on this "council of God," read *The Unseen Realm* by Michael S. Heiser.

Part One: Satan's Origin and History

After mankind was created and some of them had died, the council was enlarged to include representatives of the human saints who had died.

God tells this council what He wants done and allows the council members to have input, but then God decrees what He wants done and lets the council members decide how to best implement His will. For example, a company has an owner, a CEO, or a top executive who calls the shot. Those in the next tier under him offer advice to the leader on what he hopes or wishes the company to accomplish. Those top employees do what must be done to achieve the selected goals. ***This business example is a simplistic way to explain God's council and how it functions under His control.***

Would it be fair to ask the question: *"Is the idea of God's having a council biblical?"*

First, to answer the question if there is indeed a divine council, starting at the very beginning of the Bible in the book of Genesis is a must. I will provide several biblical references, but for a larger list of Bible verses, as well as a better understanding of them, consulting the book I have already mentioned, *The Unseen Realm* by Michael S. Heir, would be most helpful.

In Genesis 1:28 the Lord makes the statement, *"Let us make man in our own image."* The $64 question is to whom is God speaking when He refers to "us"? In Psalm 82:1 David writes that God stands in the congregation of the mighty where He judges among the lesser gods. The Bible refers to these lesser gods as angels who were probably the original council members.

In Matthew 19:28 Jesus told the disciples that they would reign with Him in heaven. If so, either the council members will be changed, or the council will be expanded.

The psalmist in Psalm 89:5-7 asks, *"Who is like the* LORD *among heavenly beings?* **In the council of the holy ones, God is greatly feared....**" (In plain words, in the council, God is the top one.)

Daniel writes in the seventh chapter regarding his vision of the Ancient of Days (v. 10), **the court was seated,** and the books were opened. That would be a direct reference to God's court on duty. Again, in Daniel 7:26 (NKJV) the prophet writes, *"****But the court shall be seated,*** *and they shall take away his dominion...."* (The *dominion* referenced is the domain of Satan and his fallen angels.)

In the fourteenth chapter of Isaiah, Satan is quoted saying, "I will ascend to heaven and rule the angels. I will take the highest throne. I will preside on the **Mount of Assembly** far away in the North."

This "mount of assembly" is the one where the heavenly council convened here on earth. Some theologians say this mount is on Earth, while others believe it is in heaven. Others believe there is a mountain where the council met located in each place, and that viewpoint makes the most sense. I would think that after Satan was cast out of heaven, the earthly meeting place was no longer used by God.

Jeremiah 23:18 (KJV) states it in this manner: *"For who has stood in the* **counsel** *of the* LORD, *and has perceived and heard his word?"*

The final Scripture reference listed in this book is found in Job 15:8 (NIV). Job is asked, *"Do you listen in on God's* **council?** *Do you have a monopoly on wisdom?"*

John, in the book of Revelation, refers several times to the 24 elders sitting on thrones. I have often wondered about those statements, but now I think they refer to a **council within the council.** In other words, they are the head council.

Several additional verses can be found referring to God's council, but those I have shared are enough for the purposes of this book to show the prestige of Satan. He was close enough to God Himself that he would be allowed to sit on this council. Satan was so close and intimate with God that it is now easier to understand how he thought he could usurp God's angels, and even take over God's throne.

> **But how Satan thought he could be equal with God is incomprehensible.**

Part 1:4
Satan's Rebellion

Satan was on the heavenly council when God suggested the earthly creation. Satan probably had no problem with this desire of God. Satan probably advised God and possibly even helped in the creation planning.

God said the humans would be created a little lower than the angels for a time, after which they would rule the angels. Satan then saw his high position being usurped by those whom he considered to be inferior.

I once read the following saying: *"Satan would rather reign in hell than serve in heaven."* This attitude could have been the catalyst that set the seeds of rebellion aflame in Satan.

Creation took place, and Adam and Eve were created. We will not know this side of heaven how long after creation Satan finally put his plan of seduction with Eve into place.

However, given that Adam had to name all the animals and Eve had to be created, it would be reasonable to assume the temptation did not take place immediately.

Side note here: snakes were not then as they are today. They were not repulsive, *and Eve did not seem to be surprised by conversing with this animal. Before God cursed snakes, most likely they did not crawl on the ground.* For Satan's misrepresentation of the snake, God's punishment included their being repulsive to mankind, as well as crawling on the ground.

Isaiah 14:12-14 (NKJV) opens the text given the title of **"The Fall of Lucifer."** I find it easy to understand the TLB translation, so that is the translation printed.

> *How you are fallen from heaven, O Lucifer, son of the morning! How you are cut down to the ground—mighty though you were against the nations of the world.* [13]*For you said to yourself, "I will ascend to heaven and rule the angels. I will take the highest throne. I will preside on the Mount of Assembly far away in the north.* [14]*I will climb to the highest heavens and be like the Most High."*

Reading this passage clearly reveals that pride brought Satan down. Satan's higher title of *Lucifer* is also used in this passage. From the standpoint of time in God's eyes, Satan was brought down when he first entertained the sin of pride.

However, Satan was not removed from heaven at this time. And Satan either wanted to continue to sit on the earthly council or expects to get back on the Council of the North, which is located here on earth.

My thinking is that Satan kept the council location located on earth but staffed it with his fallen hierarchy of angels.

Until Satan was physically removed from heaven, it would appear from the passage in Zechariah that he continued to spend time in heaven accusing the saints of God.

"Then he showed me Joshua the high priest standing before the Angel of the Lord, and Satan standing at his right hand to oppose him. ²And the Lord said to Satan, "The Lord rebuke you, Satan! The Lord who has chosen Jerusalem rebuke you! Is this not a brand plucked from the fire?" (Zechariah 3:1-2 NKJV).

Apparently, Satan was still physically allowed in heaven when John wrote the book of Revelation. John saw Satan bound and cast into the pit where he was confined to keep him from deceiving the nations for a time. Not until the ascension of Jesus, when He completely overcame Satan, would this passage in Zechariah explain how Satan could still be in heaven making accusations.

Interesting that Jesus in Luke 10:18b (KJV) said to the 70 that He had sent out, *"I beheld Satan as lightning fall from heaven."* (The Greek tense of these words would read somewhat differently. In the Greek, the text would read, "I was beholding Satan as he fell.")

There is no question that Satan fell or that he has been cast out of heaven. The only question about this event was the sequence, and the time frame to accomplish Satan's total removal.

In Revelation 2:9 John declares that war broke out in heaven between Michael and his angels who fought against Satan and his angels. Satan and his angels lost and were cast out of heaven.

Following this war, a voice was heard heralding the defeat of the Accuser.

Part 1:5
Biblical Names of Satan

1) *Satan* is the most used name in the Bible and the one that is best recognized as God's enemy. This name, which is used 52 times in

the Word of God, means "adversary." He is the enemy of God who opposes what God does and all that God loves. The opposition includes opposition to God and the angels still in heaven, as well as to all humans but especially toward Christians.

2) ***Lucifer***, which is used in Isaiah 14, is the name used to address the king of Babylon. But the description of Lucifer seems to fit a more powerful king or Satan—the logical choice. ***Lucifer*** means "morning star" and is used to describe a being who sought to overthrow God's very throne.

3) ***Guardian Cherub***, which appears in Ezekiel 28, is used to describe the king of Tyre. But like the passage in Isaiah, this name appears to go far beyond the description of a mere mortal who was laid low by pride. This name could also be another one for "Guardian Angel"— the name God gave the angel at His creation.

4) ***Devil* is the name used several times in the New Testament to explain Satan.** The word means "false accuser" or "slanderer." Satan plays the role of a slanderer in Job when he attacks Job's character.

5) ***Beelzebub*** is the name the Jewish people use to refer to Satan. This name means the "Lord of the Fly."

Satan also has other titles such as ***tempter, the wicked one,*** and ***accuser of the brethren.*** Three titles point to Satan's authority in this world.

- In I Corinthians 4:4, Satan is referred to as *"the god of this age."*
- In Ephesians 2:2, Satan is referred to as the *"prince of the power of the air."*
- 2 Corinthians 11:14, Satan transforms himself into *"an angel of light,"* a name which highlights his ability and inclination to deceive.

The Bible also uses several metaphors to reveal the character of the Evil One.

- In the parable of the four soils, Jesus likens Satan to the birds that snatch the seed from the hardened ground (Matthew 13:4, 19).
- In another parable, Satan appears as the sower of weeds among the wheat (Matthew 13:25, 28).
- John 10:12 compares Satan to a wolf.
- I Peter 5:8 compares Satan to a weakened, impotent, roaring lion.
- Revelation 12:9 calls Satan *"the great dragon…that serpent of old."*

Reading this section on the names of Satan should give you pause when thinking how Satan can oppress you, harass you, lie to you, deceive you, and according to John 10:10, even kill you.

Keep these names and descriptions in mind to help you know with whom and how you are really in conflict. Be aware in both your life personally and within your family members when engaging in the battle against Satan.

Part 1:6
Satan's Revolt Against God Spreads

When the rebellion of Satan actually took place is unknown, but the first couple of verses in the sixth chapter of Genesis seems to indicate the rebellion in heaven could no longer be consigned to Satan alone. Genesis 6:1-4 (TLB) makes an interesting read.

*"Now a population explosion took place upon the earth. It was at this time that **beings from the spirit world** looked*

upon the beautiful Earth women and took any they desired to be their wives."

For more comprehensive reading of this event, many additional details are found in *The Lost Book of Enoch: A Comprehensive Transliteration of the Forgotten Book of the Bible*. As you read this book, you will find many other questions answered in greater detail than in the Bible. An extensively rich background is provided much like reading the books of Josephus. This historian wrote about the destruction of Jerusalem, the razing of the Temple, the destruction of the Jewish religion, as well as the end of the Jewish tribes of Israel.

The Lost Book of Enoch adds meat to the first few verses found in Genesis 6. This book tells about the 200 angels that agreed together to come to earth with the express intention of choosing women to take as wives. They not only took wives but impregnated them, and they bore offspring. These evil angels then taught the women and their offspring what God did not want humans to know.

The Lost Book of Enoch then reveals that these 200 angels were later sorry for what they had done and asked Enoch to intercede with God on their behalf. They wanted to return to heaven. Enoch did as they asked, but God refused to let them come back, instead consigning them to hell. 2 Peter 2:4 (KJV), *"God spared not the angels that sinned, but cast them down to hell, and delivered them into chains of darkness...."*

Any good reference Bible will redirect the reader of 2 Peter 2:4-6 back to Genesis 6. The Bible says that these "half-breed" children continued to multiply in great numbers, producing giants of considerable strength and cunning. Due to their greatly expanding numbers, their size and strength, they began to take over the earth.

God had a council meeting and declared something must be done.

Part One: Satan's Origin and History

Genesis 6:3-7 explains God's attitude toward this mixed breed now peopling the earth.

> *And the LORD said, "My spirit shall not strive with man forever, for he is indeed flesh; yet his days shall be one hundred and twenty years." ⁴There were giants on the earth in those days, and also afterward, when the sons of God came in to the daughters of men and they bore children to them. Those were the mighty men who were of old, men of renown.*
>
> *⁵Then the LORD saw that the wickedness of man was great in the earth, and that every intent of the thoughts of his heart was only evil continually. ⁶And the LORD was sorry that He had made man on the earth, and He was grieved in His heart. ⁷So the LORD said, "I will destroy man whom I have created from the face of the earth, both man and beast, creeping things and birds of the air, for I am sorry I made them"* (Genesis 6:3-7 NKJV).

For comparison's sake, I will include the TLB translation:

> *Now a population explosion took place upon the earth. It was at this time that beings from the spirit world looked upon the beautiful earth women and took any they desired to be their wives. ³Then Jehovah said, "My Spirit must not forever be disgraced in man, wholly evil as he is. I will give him 120 years to mend his ways."*
>
> *⁴In those days, and even afterward, when the evil beings from the spirit world were sexually involved with human women, their children became giants, of whom so many legends are told. ⁵When Lord God saw the extent of human wickedness, and that the trend and direction of men's lives were only towards evil, ⁶he was sorry he had made them. It broke His heart* (Genesis 6:1-6 TLB).

Part 1:7
God's Destruction of His Wonderful Creation

The 120 years mentioned in the next verses were used by Noah to build an ark, and he received instructions from God. The passage concludes that **Noah** did "according to all that God commanded him" (Genesis 6:22).

The reference in this Scripture passage of Noah's genealogy was meant to imply that his generational history had never involved any mixed relations with any offspring of the fallen angels. When Scripture says that Noah and his sons were the only righteous people left, making that distinction was the full purpose

The Scripture did not mean that only Noah was righteous; rather, only that his ancestry was uncontaminated.

God's plan then was for the believers who died in the flood to die but then were taken to heaven. That transition then as now is simply a relocation of the person into a new, uncontaminated, heavenly body.

The believers who were right with God and living at the time of the flood, died and went to be with God. The remainder who did not believe in God or were unrighteous will await the final judgement somewhere.

Neither the Bible, nor the book of Enoch, provide any information of how some of these evil angelic offspring survived the flood, **but some of those giants remained on the earth,** and they again proliferated as was seen when Israel invaded the Promised Land of Canaan.

For years I could never understand **why a loving God gave the command to the Israelites to totally wipe out certain kingdoms.**

Only after researching material for this book did I finally understood what God was doing. These polluted mixed breed beings traced their lineage back to the original group of angels that had traveled to earth and taken wives of the earthly women. These remaining giants were not destroyed in the flood.

What the flood had not totally accomplished, God now instructed the Israelites to finish the job by means of a total extermination.

Part 1:8
Meanwhile, What Was Happening in Heaven?

As I have already stated, on earth, the fallen angels' offspring were polluting and corrupting the earth and everything in it. But in heaven Satan was still observed going from earth to heaven and reporting to God how bad man was.

Whether Satan still retained his place on the Council of God, or if he was simply reporting back to God and accusing God's people, we don't know. What we do know is that he was still actively engaged in persuading other angels to join with him in his goal to supplant God's authority. And if possible, he would like to take over full control…**or to at least to reign equally with God.**

Satan was still commanding respect and authority in the book of Daniel when he hindered the messenger of God. Other places in the Old Testament reveal that even high-ranking angels of God did not dispute with him personally. They simply said, *"The Lord rebuke you."*

Many angels—probably millions and millions—were originally created, but more than likely, the number was in the billions.

Assuming John was correct, a third of all the created angels chose to unite with Satan—many angels chose to rebel with Satan. Ultimately, at some time or another, those angels either followed or preceded Satan's being cast out of heaven.

We can be certain plenty of satanic workers are tempting and harassing the Christians here on earth. Those fallen angels had all the bad characteristics of Satan himself. Satan was referred to as "the father of lies," but his followers were not far behind him.

What amazes me is that God not only gave the angelic created beings the freedom to choose to follow Him or to choose to follow Satan, but He also gave that same "freedom of choice" to all mankind. **God knowing all the things that would take place with the created angels still chose to create mankind with the same freedom of choice!**

A Few Interesting Observations

The controversies regarding Satan have continued over the years. Martin Luther taught that rather than argue with Satan, Christians should avoid temptation altogether by **seeking out pleasant company. Luther especially** recommended music as a safeguard against temptation, **since the Devil cannot endure gaiety.**

Luther even advocated the removal of the book of Revelation from the Bible because he did not like the references to the Devil that were found there.

John Calvin was overheard repeating a maxim from St. Augustine saying, "Man is like a horse, with either God or the devil as rider."

The difference between the two riders is that God will gently control you with a gentle tug on the reins or a nudge, or He will have the Holy Spirit speak softly in your ear. Satan, however, uses a sharp, cutting bit in the mouth to direct you where he wants you to go, uses a riding crop cruelly applied, and screams so loud that you can hear nothing else.

A poll conducted in 1920 indicated 57 percent of the people in the

United States believed in a literal Devil. And 51 percent of Americans also believe Satan has the power to possess people. This statistic could be because over the past 40 to 50 years, Americans and even Christians, got their information from the movies—not from the Bible.

Who controls the movie industry is no secret!

For many years, the Catholic church generally played down exorcisms, especially in the late twentieth and early twenty-first century.

Pope Francis brought renewed focus on the Devil when he stated the Devil is intelligent. He went on to say that Satan knows more theology than all the theologians combined. All major religions include a Satan or a Satan "look-alike" in their beliefs.

Part One of the book, *Father God, the Devil, and You* now comes to an end.

I trust you have learned about Father God and the created angelic realm as well as some concepts about the created angel who later transitioned from the highest angelic being to be the leader of the fallen angelic realm, *and is now God's greatest enemy.*

Hopefully, you also picked up on some ideas that were new to you and will further investigate these claims rather than just shuffling them off.

The next section, Part II will address your God-given authority over Satan and his fallen angelic realm. Buckle up and learn how you, as a believer in Christ, can become a winner.

And you won't even have to wait until you get to heaven!

PART TWO

Father God, the Devil, and You

Your Authority Over the Enemy

Your Authority Over the Enemy

Part 2:9
God, and God Alone, is Supreme

Before considering our authority over Satan and his cohorts, we need to first consider who is providing the authority. The "who" is God Himself—the ultimate authority!

I have already mentioned that when the word "God" is used, the word embodies three: **God the Father, God the Son, and God the Holy Spirit.**

The source to support the claim that God is the Supreme Being, the Provider of all authority, the Creator of all, is **the Holy Bible.** If you cannot agree that the Bible is the inspired Word from God Himself, you will have a difficult time accepting what is written within these pages. *Before you blow away the use of the inspired Bible as my authority, please hear me out.*

The Bible is not just one book; it is a collection of 66 books written over a period of 1500 years. Obviously, with a time span this long, most of these authors never knew each other. These 66 individual books are a collection of history, poetry, prophecy, wisdom, literature, letters, and apocalyptic. Forty different authors of these various books came from a variety of backgrounds, including shepherds, fishermen, doctors, kings, and prophets. The books were also written in three different languages on three different continents.

History has proven these 66 books contain no historical errors or contradictions and they share a common storyline: the creation, the fall, and the redemption. **Find me another book, or a collection of books, meeting this criterion, and I will withdraw the source of my authority and rewrite this book.**

You alone will have to make your choice whether or not you will accept the Bible as a legitimate authority. Even the choice to accept Jesus as the part of the Godhead Who died, rose from the dead, and then ascended into heaven is a personal choice every human being has to make. The decision you make concerning whether to accept the Bible as inspired by God Himself and should be believed is also **your personal choice to make.** The following Scriptures support and give evidence on Who God is:

> *"The* LORD *has established His throne in the heavens, and His kingdom rules over all"* (Psalm 103:19 NKJV).

> *"Yet I* **[God]** *have set My King* **[Jesus]** *on My holy hill of Zion. I will declare the decree; the* LORD *has said to Me, You are My Son, today I have begotten You. Ask of Me, and I will give You the nations for Your inheritance, and the ends of the earth for Your possession"* (Psalm 2:6-8 NKJV).

> *"The Lord has made everything for his own purposes—even the wicked for punishment"* (Proverbs 16:4 TLB).

> *"Ah, Sovereign* LORD, *you have made the heavens and the earth by your great power and outstretched arm.* **Nothing** *is too hard for you"* (Jeremiah 32:17 NIV).

> *"Through him all things were made; without Him nothing was made that has been made. ⁴In him was life, and that life was the light of all mankind"* (John 1:3-4 NIV).

> *"For by Him all things were created that are in heaven that are on earth, visible and invisible, whether thrones or dominions or principalities or powers. All things were created through Him and for Him. ¹⁷And He is before all things, and in Him all things consist"* (Colossians 1:16-17 NKJV).

> *and said: "O Lord God of our fathers, are You not God in heaven, and do You not rule over all the kingdoms of the nations, and in Your hand is there not power and might, so that no one is able to withstand You?"* (2 Chronicles 20:6 NKJV).

> *"You are worthy, O Lord, to receive glory and honor and power; for You created all things, and by Your will they exist and were created"* (Revelation 4:11 NKJV).

> *"For from him and through him and to him are all things. To him be glory forever. Amen."* (Romans 11:36 ESV).

> *"And don't forget the many times I clearly told you what was going to happen in the future. **For I am God**—I only—and there is no other like me"* (Isaiah 46:9 TLB).

These selected verses from the Word of God represent only a few of those that put into perspective the fact that God is supreme. He made the heavens and everything in them, and He created this earth and everything in it.

Everything that you think, everything you know, or everything you even suspect was created by God and exists for His glory.

Assuming He created all things, I would suggest that He has the AUTHORITY to back up anything He says.

PART TWO: YOUR AUTHORITY OVER THE ENEMY

Part 2:10
What Is Authority?

Webster defines *authority* as "delegated power"; and in Matthew 28:18b, Jesus said, *"**All authority** has been given to Me...."*

This book, *Father God, the Devil, and You*, tells about your authority over the Enemy, Satan. I want to start from that perspective.

In Luke, Jesus tells the believer what His authority is when He said, *"And I have given you authority over all the power of the Enemy, and to walk among serpents and scorpions and to crush them. **Nothing** shall injure you!"* (Luke 10:19 TLB). Before dissecting this verse, I want to address a simple question. Do you think the church of the Lord Jesus Christ needs any less **authority and power** over the evil demonic realm today than it did in the first century?

Or is it reality that the church (which means **you**) probably needs to use the power more today because Satan has become more entrenched in the church over the years because of his lies and deceit?

Jesus said in the passage that He is the One Who has power over the Devil. And that power was so great and so all-sufficient that the believers would tread on the serpent (the Devil) and on scorpions (the fallen angels).

When people (including Christians) in the Western world evaluate what happens in their life, they do so only at the human level. Examples of what I mean would include wars, arguments (**within families**), accidents, natural disasters, and so forth. Isn't the first thing we look for is a reason for what is happening or has happened?

What did we do at the onset of the Covid-19 pandemic? We tried to find a cause or something to blame it on. Christians need to ask God if they are missing something He is trying to tell them.

Christians especially need to consider that an important supernatural aspect could be involved as well.

When reading the Old Testament, how often *didn't* God use natural causes in nature to punish nations? **How often *didn't* God use other nations to punish the Jews?**

Take the flood, for instance. God said He was sending the flood to destroy the world because of the evil influence of the off-breed children that the angels and the earthly women had created. The flood would be an instance of supernatural input from the spirit realm—both from God and Satan.

How often in the Old Testament *didn't* God say the punishment was more than He was happy with? *In those cases Satan's involvement increased God's desired punishment.*

One of the questions that will be addressed is whether the Enemy gets involved in human sickness and disease. In John 10:10 (NIV), Jesus put it very plainly when He stated profoundly: *"The thief comes only to steal and kill and destroy...."*

And again in the TLB translation, the passage reads, *"The thief's purpose is to steal, kill and destroy...."*

The church has forgotten the words of Jesus, and Satan has fooled the Christians and gained the upper hand.

A quick review of history, as well as currently, should leave no doubt in our mind that these words regarding the Devil come directly from Jesus and should be taken literally.

Christians in the Western world generally think they have a theological understanding about Satan and his demons, but that knowledge very seldom leads to a functional faith in dealing with the incidents.

Christians can also go too far in seeing demons involved in every problem. And Christians can also give more power and influence to the demonic world than warranted.

However, for the most part the parishioners in Christian churches go in the other direction. **They pretend there is no demonic involvement,** or *Christians pretend the Devil cannot touch them as they have the Holy Spirit in them.*

A spiritual point that is often overlooked in the discussion regarding God and Satan is the fact that **God and Satan are *not* equals.** Satan would certainly like mankind to believe he is equal with God, *but in reality, the Devil is simply another created being.*

The prophet Hosea wrote that God Himself had said: *"My people are destroyed for lack of knowledge..."* (4:6 NKJV).

The authors of the TLB translation stated this verse so much more bluntly: *"My people are destroyed because they don't know me, and it is all your fault, you priests, for you yourselves refuse to know me; therefore, I refuse to recognize you as my priests. Since you have forgotten my laws, I will 'forget' to bless your children"* (Hosea 4:6 TLB).

In John 8 Jesus said: *"And you shall know the truth, and the truth shall make you free"* (John 8:32 NKJV).

How is a Christian to know the truth? Where can the truth be found? Those are two very good questions with an easy answer. The Christian can find the truth in God's Word.

The problem is that the Enemy can confuse the truth. However, if you will start reading the Word by asking the Holy Spirit, in Jesus' name, to guide you into all truth, you will not be led astray (John 8:32 NKJV).

Always remember, **your** authority over Satan and his kingdom rests on the power of Jesus Christ, Who died, rose again, and ascended into heaven. Then God put **ALL** the Enemy under Him.

God can be very blunt, and He can be very direct, but He is God. He is direct so you may give Him the glory that He deserves.

Part 2:11
What Is the Christian's Authority?

Authority is "delegated power." Jesus is the head of the church, and **you** as a believer and a member of Jesus Christ's church, are a part of His body. As a member of His body, **you** now have His authority over the Devil, as well as over the rest of His kingdom.

Jesus has provided you with His authority. He has also promised you the POWER of His name whenever **you** use that authority over Satan, which **means the authority and the power of His name is active every time you use it.**

It would be obvious to anyone who takes the time to look and evaluate the body of Christ, today's church seems to have missed the promise. So, the question to be asked is as follows:

Does the Christian have any God-given authority over Satan and his demonic realm about which he does not know, has not yet discovered, or that the body of Christ in general, is not using?
In this section, the author will use the Word to establish the Christian's authority and power over Satan.

This biblical journey begins with Ephesians 1:20-23, where Paul tells us that God raised Christ from the dead and proceeded to seat Jesus in heaven at His right hand. Of interest to note is that in the kingdoms at that time, the king's throne was built to seat two people. The extra place was for the person the king wished to honor. This explanation would clarify the various passages mentioning Jesus being seated beside God.

[Christ is seated] — *"Far above all principality and power and might and dominion, and every name that is named, not only in this age but also in that which is to come. ²²And He put all things under His feet, and gave Him to be head over all things to the church, ²³which is His body, the fullness of Him who fills all in all"* (Ephesians 1:21-23 NKJV).

In the second chapter of Ephesians Paul expands on the passage from the first chapter when he wrote under the guidance of the Holy Spirit: "[God] *made us alive together with Christ…⁶and raised us up together, and made us sit together in the heavenly places in Christ Jesus"* (Ephesians 2:5b-6 NKJV).

Part 2:12
Your God-Given Authority Over Satan and His Spiritual Realm

In Ephesians 1:18-23 Paul told of the great power that is available to the Christian. He goes on to tell how that **great power** is greater than all the evil rulers, dictators, and leaders.

Paul continues to tell us that Christ has all things under His feet, but Paul did not stop there; he puts the believer in **His Church** right there with Him.

> *"I pray that your hearts will be flooded with light so that you can see something of the future he has called you to share. I want you to realize that God has been made rich because we who are Christ's have been given to him! ¹⁹I pray that you will begin to understand how incredibly great his power is to help those who believe him. It is the same mighty power ²⁰that raised Christ from*

the dead and seated him in the place of honor at God's right hand in heaven, ^{21}far, far above any other king or ruler or dictator or leader. ^{22}Yes, his honor is far more glorious than that of anyone else either in this world or on the world to come. ^{22}And God has put all things under his feet and made Him the supreme Head of the Church—^{23}which is his body, filled with himself, the Author and Giver of everything everywhere" (Ephesians 1:18–23 TLB).

This passage is so potent and full of knowledge. Let me unpack some of the truths contained in this Scripture. First, Paul wants your heart to be open and filled with the light from the Holy Spirit so you can begin to realize some of your great future in Jesus. **And that puts you above Satan and his evil realm.** Then Paul informs you that God is the One made rich because **you** belong to Christ, and because **you** do belong to Christ, God will give you the same great power He has bestowed upon Jesus!

In heaven, God has seated Jesus beside Him, far above the evil realm of Satan. *If that wasn't enough, He has seated you right along with Christ as Head of the Church in heaven.*

The church Jesus heads is not some earthly entity or denomination. Jesus is the Head of the true church composed of those who have trusted Him and invited Him into their life. Because you are in Christ, **you** are seated with Him in heaven alongside of God Who provides you with certain rights. **You** belong to Christ, and God has given the church, of which **you** are a member, to Jesus.

Then because Christ is seated in heaven as the head of the church, Jesus has passed on His authority over Satan and His dominion to the church. **Jesus has backed up His "Power of Attorney" to you, along with all His power over Satan.**

Part Two: Your Authority Over the Enemy

The Christian's authority is often overlooked, and in truth, most churches and pastors don't even acknowledge that Satan exists. *Neither do they know or teach that the believer has any authority over Satan*—much less what, how, and when Satan afflicts the Christian. I will share more on that aspect in Part III.

In a casual look at the churches of today, we must wonder what happened to all the power and/or authority that was given to Jesus following His death and resurrection. There is no question that Jesus is the Head of His church. Another given is that Jesus is now in heaven.

The question is: did Jesus simply take all His earthly power that He had available when He was here to heaven with Him? Did He leave His church hanging in the breeze? **Or has His church that remains in the body here on earth failed to appropriate the God-given authority and power that Scripture teaches Jesus made available to His church?**

Assuming I am reading the Scriptures correctly, Jesus the Head of the church remains in heaven, while the body functions on earth. The Head tells the body what has to be done, how it has to be done, and then provides the authority and power to do so.

When a person becomes one with Christ, even though the body remains for a time on earth, the real person is in heaven with Jesus Christ.

A little side note here: the death of Jesus was engineered by Satan, and he used human entities, i.e., *the Jewish rulers, the Romans, and Judas*, he controlled.

The resurrection of Jesus not only caught Satan by surprise but also caused his total defeat. In the book of Revelation, John tells his readers that Satan was not only thrown out of heaven, he was bound up in the pit so that he could no longer deceive nations.

All Satan and his dominion can do now is harass, intimidate, deceive, cause sickness, cause the physical death of mankind, but especially of Christians. He wants to steal your joy, your health, and everything else. **Additionally, whenever he has the opportunity, he will also steal your life.**

The next part of the book will examine in more detail the impact Satan can have on sickness, and yes, even death.

Part 2:13
Your Authority Is a Delegated Authority

We have touched on what authority is, and we established that your authority both directly and indirectly comes from God Himself.

Biblically, there can be no argument that Jesus died, was made alive, and then went to Heaven where He sits at the right hand of God.

In reading the Bible, there should be no question that Satan was behind the entire 39 stripes that Jesus bore on His back, the suffering, the humiliation, and finally His crucifixion. If Satan could have removed Jesus from the picture, he would have been in total control on this earth. Sickness, lack of health, and through death which he had *and has under his control.* **Father God had other plans of which Satan was not aware. God's power over death gave life back to His Son, and in the process totally defeated Satan and the other fallen angels.**

In the process of the resurrection, God seated Jesus in heaven far above the evil realm. God gave Jesus the defeated evil realm and tells us that Jesus is now seated far above all Satan's domain.

Let's review the delegated process so far. God's power raised Jesus from the death that Satan had engineered. God then delegated to Jesus the power over Satan and all the evil ones.

Part Two: Your Authority Over the Enemy

The next step in the delegated power process is when Christ passes on to His church the power over Satan that had been passed on to Him by God.

Paul wrote in Ephesians 2:1-8 (NKJV) that when you accepted Jesus as your Savior, you died, but then you were raised with Christ, and **God now sees you seated in heaven with Him.**

> *"And you He made alive, who were dead in trespasses and sins, ²in which you once walked according to the course of this world, according to the prince of the power of the air, the spirit who now works in the sons of disobedience, ³among whom also we all once conducted ourselves in the lusts of our flesh, fulfilling the desires of the flesh and of the mind, and were by nature children of wrath just as the others.*
>
> *⁴But God, who is rich in mercy, because of His great love with which He loved us, ⁵even when we were dead in trespasses, made us alive together with Christ (by grace you have been saved) ⁶and raised us up together, and made us sit together in the heavenly places in* [or with] *Christ Jesus, ⁷that in the ages to come He might show the exceeding riches of His grace in His kindness toward us in Christ Jesus. ⁸For by grace you have been saved through faith, and that not of yourselves; it is the gift of God"* (Ephesians 2:1-8 NKJV).

Okay, you are now made alive—just as Christ was. You sit in heaven with Jesus. You, through Christ, are over the evil realm of Satan—just as Jesus is. The process of delegation runs from God to Jesus.

Jesus is Head of His church, and He has now delegated His power to the body. As the Head, Jesus directs and supplies the power, but **you, the body, must now do the actual work.**

You will never understand with your intellect this spiritual truth. You must get the spiritual revelations of this truth from the Holy Spirit and by reading God's Word. Then after gaining your personal knowledge and understanding, you must believe it by faith. (See Ephesians 2:1-7, 1 Corinthians 12:14-17, 2 Corinthians 6:14-15.)

Jesus is the Head of the church, and **you** are a part of His body, **you** have His authority, and **you** may use the power of His name—the name of Jesus to defeat the Enemy **every time!**

Delegated POWER does not come
with any greater POWER!

Part 2:14
Your Authority Is Now

Jesus said in Matthew 28:18b (NKJV), *"All authority has been given to Me in heaven and on earth."*

Again Jesus said in Luke 10:18b-19 (TLB), *"I saw Satan falling from heaven as a flash of lightning!* ¹⁹*And I have given you authority over all the power of the Enemy, and to walk among serpents and scorpions and to crush them...."*

Jesus is the Head, and He supplies the power to the church; **He has entrusted His saints with His authority over Satan's realm.**

Jesus died for us, and after dying for us, He was raised back to life, defeating Satan in the process. He then made the power of His resurrection available to us.

In legal terms that transaction is known as **"Power of Attorney."** By granting you and me His power of attorney, Jesus literally gave us all His power over Satan and his realm.

The two kinds of power of attorney are a "Limited Power of Attorney" and an "Unlimited Power of Attorney." In dealing with Satan and his realm, we have both in that Jesus has given us His **unlimited** power when it comes to dealing with Satan, but that unlimited power is **limited** to our dealings with Satan.

Part 2:15
Each Encounter and for Every Time

Jesus made it very clear in Mark 16 that **the authority to use His unlimited power was for the time of the disciples. It would seem that it was not going to go away.** Jesus said the following to them:

"Go into all the world and preach the gospel to every creature. ¹⁶He who believes and is baptized will be saved; but he who does not believe will be condemned. ¹⁷And these signs will follow those who believe: **in My name they will cast out demons;** *they will speak with new tongues; ¹⁸they will take up serpents; and if they drink anything deadly, it will by no means hurt them; they will lay hands on the sick, and they will recover"* (Mark 16:15b-18 NKJV).

And in the Living Bible translation, we read:

"You are to go into all the world and preach the Good News to everyone, everywhere. ¹⁶Those who believe and are baptized will be saved. But those who refuse to believe will be condemned. ¹⁷And **those who believe shall use my authority to cast out demons,** *and they shall speak new languages. ¹⁸They will be able even to handle snakes with safety, and if they drink anything*

poisonous, it won't hurt them; and they will place their hands on the sick and heal them" (Mark 16:15b-18 TLB).

I included both versions to a make the point *that* different versions of Mark 16 will say virtually the same thing. I would like to draw your attention to a couple of things. The passage referring to the Great Commission is greatly expanded in Mark from the passage found in Matthew.

Very seldom in a church service where the pastor is preaching on the Great Commission is the passage in Mark used. My assumption is that most pastors of churches don't want to address healing, and most pastors will not talk about the Devil, how to cast him out, or *the saint's authority over him.*

If the passage in Matthew is used, then the church can talk about winning souls, giving away food, providing clothes, and going on mission trips to build homes. **Preaching the good news is the only common denominator found in both passages.** Anyone can give away food and clothes, build houses, etc., and by doing so, they can feel good about themselves. These things, mostly by inference can be found in the Bible, but they were not included in the words of Jesus at the time of His ascension. **It could be that the church has majored on the minor and minored on the major.**

My assumption on why the passage from Matthew is used is so the preacher can then pretend only the words in Matthew are needed **or are prevalent.** *However, the reality is that the charges found in Mark are also found throughout the New Testament,* **and that makes the words in Mark legitimate.**

Shame on those churches and their pastors! They are willing to go and to win souls for Jesus with the promise of eternal life, *which has to be taken by faith.* **But they are not willing to trust Jesus for healing or in dealing with the evil ones in the here and now. Do you, or they, think it takes a different kind of faith to believe Jesus for eternity than it does for healing or deliverance?**

You have probably never thought that the cross is actually a place of defeat. *If the resurrection had not occurred, Satan would have won!* The stripes that Jesus bore on His back at Calvary for our healing would have meant nothing if Jesus had not ascended into heaven. The victory that Jesus won over Satan with His resurrection would not have happened. *Jesus' ascension to heaven was what caused the defeat of the cross and turned it into a throne religion.*

Ask yourself, what religion you are hearing preached? **Did the preaching of the cross stop when Jesus went to heaven? Are Christians supposed to stop at the cross?** *Should the preaching and teaching for healing and deliverance stop because Jesus left the earth?* **Does the Christian need healing and deliverance now or when he gets to heaven?**

Is what you are hearing in your church, the religion that Jesus preached while He was on earth? *Or has that true religion Jesus preached and demonstrated been watered down?*

Somewhere I heard a saying that went like this: "**Preach the Word, and if necessary, use words.**"

It is right now when **you** are hurting and when **you** are being destroyed that **you** need the authority and power that Jesus purchased for **you**. **Is it easier for you to accept salvation and eternal life by faith without seeing it until you die?** This is a promised gift that you are willing to take by faith and one that you do not totally receive or experience until you die.

Why is the faith to believe for deliverance and healing by faith different than the faith you need for your eternal heritage? Is it because *you would see the benefits of your faith now; and if you don't see the results of your faith, you might then doubt your faith?*

It takes the same faith to believe for your salvation and eternal life, as it does to believe for healing and deliverance. And in all honesty, that salvation faith also comes from the same Holy Spirit, *and also comes by asking.*

The only difference is that you will see and realize the evidence of your trust and faith before you arrive in heaven! Do you think that if you saw healing take place in your life, or in the life of one of your loved ones, or if you saw the demons depart from you, **that it would increase or decrease your faith? Your authority over sin, sickness, family problems, addictions, and Satan's harassment, is not something that is yours only when you get to heaven.**

Be honest! You surely won't need the victory there. If Jesus' suffering and death were only for eternal life, **why did Jesus have to go through more than just death on the cross for your sins?**

Forgiveness of sins is separate from deliverance and healing. **You ask for each separately, and you receive each separately.** When **you come into contact with evil spirits, whether by sickness, death, temptation, or harassment, remember Jesus has defeated all the powers of evil, including Satan. You** through Christ Jesus have the same authority and power over Satan's fallen spiritual realm that Jesus has.

The Word tells us that we are in this world, but we are not of this world. This may be Satan's world, but according to God, we are seated **right now in heaven with Jesus Christ above Satan and all of Satan's rulers, principalities, powers of darkness, and fallen angels.**

You, and you alone, can decide to run from the Devil, or **you** can take the authority and power that God through Jesus offers to **you**; and **you** can defeat him in **your** life and those of **your** family.

PART TWO: YOUR AUTHORITY OVER THE ENEMY

Part 2:16
Jesus No Longer Deals Directly with the Devil

"Oh, no!" you say. "I don't believe that Jesus won't deal with the Devil for me."

Okay, why then after Jesus went to heaven, do we no longer read where He ever again dealt directly with Satan on our behalf? And if I tell you that Jesus **can no longer deal** with the Devil here on earth, I am sure you would think I have been taking stupid pills.

"What about the Lord's prayer?" you ask.

The verse in the Lord's Prayer simply states, *"And lead us not into temptation...."* (Matthew 6:13). What you are really asking is for the Father to keep you from temptation. Surely you do not think that God would lead you into temptation, do you? Neither does this prayer have anything to do with dealing with the Devil.

First, I want to address the statement that neither Jesus nor the Father are dealing directly with Satan and his evil realm for you when you pray this prayer—except in Revelation, where it is written that Satan was bound and cast into the pit. **And that passage is God's dealing with Satan in heaven, not on earth.** I challenge you to find one place in the Bible after Jesus went to heaven, where He ever again dealt, either personally or directly, with Satan.

I can hear you thinking, *that cannot be correct.*

In his book, *The Authority of the Believer,* Kenneth Hagin shared about being interrupted by a little demon who jumped around and totally interfered with his communication with God as he was praying.

Finally, Hagin became angry and told that little interfering demon to get out in Jesus' name. When he did, the demon just crumpled up and left his presence whimpering. When Kenneth resumed talking with Jesus, he asked the Savior why He didn't command that little devil to leave.

Jesus told Kenneth that He could not tell the Devil to leave.

Kenneth said to Jesus, "Surely You meant that You *would* not—not that You *could* not."

Jesus told Kenneth that He would give him a list of Bible passages to support what He had told Hagin—that He *could* not. The first Scripture Hagin was given was Matthew 28:18b (NKJV), *"All authority has been given to Me in heaven and on earth."*

When Jesus went to heaven, He went there as the Head of His church. From that point on His authority over Satan was passed on to the church.

His power through using His name was provided to enforce that authority. Jesus had died, rose again, and went to heaven, and in the process, He had totally defeated the Devil. **In other words, Jesus had done His part; from then on, it was the responsibility of the church.**

The second Scripture passage, commonly known as the Great Commission, that Jesus gave Hagin is found in Mark 16:15b-19. Read these verses again to see if you don't agree that Jesus was all done; now it is our turn. These words are also Jesus' last words to His followers and for us as well. Jesus said:

> *"****You*** *are to go into all the world and preach the Good News to everyone, everywhere.* ¹⁶*Those who believe and are baptized will be saved. But those who refuse to believe will be condemned.* ¹⁷*And* ***those who believe shall use my authority to cast out demons****, and they shall speak new languages.* ¹⁸*They will be able even to handle snakes with safety, and if they drink anything poisonous, it won't hurt them; and they will be able to place their hands on the sick and heal them"* (Mark 16:15b-18 TLB).

Part Two: Your Authority Over the Enemy

James 4:7, the next verse Jesus gave to Hagin, makes it very clear that **You** are the one who is to resist the Devil. Jesus provided the believer the authority and the power, but James makes it very clear that **YOU** are the one who will need to exercise that authority and power.

That authority is yours—whether or not you feel like you have it. The authority has nothing to do with feelings. Operating in faith has nothing to do with what you feel but in Whom you trust.

"Resist the devil and he will flee from you" (James 4:7b TLB).

The dictionary describes the significance of the word *flee* which means "to run from in terror." When you use the authority and power that Jesus has made available to you, the Devil will not only run from you, *but he will run from you in terror.*

You believed by faith and were saved. You are willing to believe that Jesus' death and resurrection has saved you for all eternity. *Are you willing to believe Him when He said He had defeated the Devil and passed that victory over the Devil on to the church* **to which you belong?**

The next reference given to Hagin is found in 1 Peter 5:8-9 (NKJV). Again, as in the former verses, the implied subject is **YOU**.

> *"Be sober, be vigilant; because your adversary the devil walks about like a roaring lion, seeking whom he may devour. Resist him, steadfast in the faith, knowing that the same sufferings are accomplished by your brotherhood in the world."*

As I have already mentioned, the subject of this interesting passage is **YOU** understood. You are to be aware of attacks from the Devil, your adversary. The interesting word in this verse is the word *as*, which is a clear understanding that Satan's power has been broken in the life of a Christian. *As* in this case means that Satan is pretending.

A lion has teeth; Satan's teeth have been removed.

A lion has claws; Satan's claws have been pulled.

A fully developed lion is very strong; Satan is feeble and has one foot in the grave.

All this *imitation* lion has left is his roar.

You, on the other hand, are wearing spiritual earmuffs and cannot hear his ineffective roar. You are also carrying a high-powered rifle, loaded and cocked, i.e., **Jesus!**

So why is the church and its members afraid of this fake lion? Yes, he is your opponent, but why are you letting him defeat you? Why is it that most Christians are running around scared and saying, "Oh, the Devil's after me!" They ask for prayer, so the Devil won't get them.

If you are praying a prayer like that, the Devil's already got you.

No, you are told by Peter, **you** are to do something about the Devil when you find yourself in a bad demonic situation. **You** have been given the authority, and Jesus will supply the power when you use that authority. Peter, who wrote under the inspiration of the Holy Spirit, would not tell **you** do something that **you** cannot do.

Jesus did His part by defeating the Devil. Now are you willing to do your part with the authority that Jesus gave you to defeat the Devil?

The real question is this: do you think that what Jesus did by dying on the cross was real? Will heaven now be your home when you die?

Are you willing to accept what Jesus did in defeating the Devil at the cross so that you can now continue His ministry here on earth?

Are you willing to trust Him to supply what He said He had supplied, and what is now yours?

Or are you going to slap Jesus on the face and call Him a liar? And that you really don't want all He has to offer?

You were willing to accept His offer to forgive your sins so you can enjoy eternity with Him in heaven. **Are you willing to accept the rest of what He is offering to you?** Are you, **by faith,** willing to accept the fact that Jesus' death and resurrection was sufficient to overcome your sins. Are you **NOT** willing to accept what He said about His death being sufficient to defeat the Devil?

Are you **NOT** willing to accept that the stripes Jesus bore on His back at Calvary were sufficient to provide you, not only with healing, **but to provide you with health as well?** *It is the same faith, and that faith for all of the earthly benefits can only come from the Holy Spirit!*

Part 2:17
Does Your God-Given Authority Extend to Others?

The answer is both a yes and a no. What do I mean?

Before a saint attempts to cast the Devil out of others, it would be well if he or she first had the knowledge of the authority in their own lives and over the lives of their family. It will be helpful to have learned to trust the power that Jesus made available to deal with the Devil, before trying to free others.

In all honesty, the average Christian will never be involved with others in the ministry of deliverance or healing. The believer may have initial success in delivering another from the clutches of the Devil, but once you leave them, you have no control over their thoughts or the conduct of their life. That is no different than your having control over their money or in the discipline of their children. **That authority belongs to them to exercise.**

How much better it would be to teach the young Christians to believe and trust Jesus for themselves. *Then they would be able to defeat the Devil in their life or in their family.*

Work with them in helping them do the actual casing out, rather than doing this for them. *Then when the Devil attacks the next time, they will know what to do and how to do it.*

Part 2:18
What Part Does Faith Play in Your Authority?

The most referred-to Bible verse on faith is found in Hebrews 11:1-3 and reads like this:

> *"Now faith is the substance of things hoped for, the evidence of things not seen. For by it the elders obtained a good testimony. By faith we understand the worlds were framed by the word of God, so that things which are seen were not made of things which are visible"* (Hebrews 11:1-3 NKJV).

> *"What is faith? It is the confident assurance that something we want is going to happen..."* (Hebrews 11:1 TLB).

You have faith that when you have worked for a certain period, your employer will pay you. That is one kind of faith, and if it doesn't come to pass when it was supposed to, you know it immediately. That is not the biblical kind of faith that a Christian must have.

The faith that a believer must have involves trusting that the One Who made the promise can be trusted to keep the promise. The passage in Hebrews lists the results of several people who had faith, but that really does not define faith very well. Those saints listed are simply stating their trust/faith and then the results of their faith.

So what exactly is faith? Everybody talks about it. Preachers preach about it, but few take time to define what that faith in the book of Hebrews really means. I probably won't do much better, but I will try.

Part Two: Your Authority Over the Enemy

Faith means "to have a complete trust, or confidence, in someone or something." An example of faith in something would be going up in an airplane to skydive. When I went skydiving a few times, I never questioned the integrity of the parachute. I knew if I pulled the ripcord, the parachute would open, and most likely, I would not get hurt.

If someone you had never known offered you a check for $100,000, you would have two choices. Is there money in the bank to cover the check? Do I trust the legitimacy of the check enough to go to the bank? But that is not the kind of faith you must have in God. Faith in God is believing Someone you have never personally met, Who has made an abundance of promises, and you will only experience one of those promises after you die.

Faith is a **complete trust and confidence** in a God Who is Who He says He is and will do what He says He will do. This faith is a strong belief in God based on a spiritual expectation, rather than seeing any proof. It is a belief not based on proof. You can hear of the faith stories that others report, but until you personally have that kind of faith experience, you have no proof.

To make it even more difficult is the fact that you have an enemy who will lie to you and tell you that you are crazy to believe that stuff.

However, you have an ace in the hole. The Holy Spirit will give you the trust you need to believe what God has said and that He is who He says He is. Faith involves exercising your spiritual authority, but don't base your faith and trust on what you feel, see or don't see, **but on what the Word says.**

When your circumstance doesn't change immediately, don't start thinking, *this won't work for you*. God may simply be testing you to see if you will keep trusting Him, instead of what you do not see happening in your circumstance. The Bible verses are very clear that you have all the authority you need to defeat the enemy called Satan. And while we are at it, you have all the promises, as well many instances where Jesus healed others to back up the healing promises.

So why not ask God to have His Holy Spirit provide you with the faith for both deliverance and healing at the same time?

God does not lie, and He even went so far as to put His promises to you in writing. **If God does not come through, ask Him what you are missing or doing wrong.**

Don't forget to listen for His answers.

Sometimes your problem with not getting an answer will relate back to the fact that you have permitted or allowed the Enemy to exist in you, and he is blocking your promised results.

What do I mean?

Are you living in some sort of sin? Then even though you have the promises and the authority, **God cannot deliver on His promises to you because sin stands between you and God Who holds the power.** And you will also have a problem dealing with the Devil as long as he can keep you in doubt and unbelief *in your mind as well as in your faith.*

Satan will work in your mind by telling you that your little sin doesn't matter. And if you are honest, **you really like that little (or even big) sin.** And since no one knows about your hidden sin, *what is the big deal?*

This is a lie from Satan, and you may think your sin is hidden, but guess who knows? The other problem with a hidden sin is when Satan has completely destroyed you, he will make sure your sin is revealed.

When you find your mind listening to Satan's lies, try demanding in the name of Jesus for the spirit of doubt to leave you.

If you find your faith to believe in the authority Jesus has promised you a little weak, ask the Holy Spirit to increase your faith to believe the promises and for Jesus to grant you the victory.

Paul recorded in Colossians a Scripture that supports the asking,

"that you may be filled with the knowledge of His will in all wisdom and spiritual understanding;...[11]*strengthened with all might, according to His glorious power...*[13]*He has delivered us from the power of darkness and conveyed us into the kingdom of the Son of His love, in whom we have redemption through His blood, the forgiveness of sins"* (Colossians 1:9b-14 NKJV).

Paul is speaking about the same Jesus Who freed you from your sins. This is the same Jesus Who has promised you eternal life. This is the same Jesus Who is now promising to give you knowledge and spiritual understanding when you encounter evil spirits.

Whether in sickness, death, temptation, or harassment; **you have the authority in Jesus.** Why do you have that authority? Because this is the same Jesus Who redeemed you from your sins. This the same Jesus Who is willing to provide you with all the things listed in the Colossians passage.

When you come into a spiritual contact with the evil spirits, whether in sickness, death, temptations, harassment, or in any other situation; *remember Jesus has defeated them.* And you through Christ Jesus have the same authority and power over these fallen angels that Jesus has.

Part 2:19
Learn to Be Exalted

Exalted means "to be lifted up." **Heaven is as high as anyone can be lifted up**; and that is where we are now—seated with Jesus in God's new heaven.

True, physically we are not in heaven, but according to the Word of God, in heaven is where Father God sees you and me—**right now.**

Our current physical location will last until we transition from this life to the next one, from this body to our new one. Then we will spend all eternity in that blessed location.

You are an ambassador from heaven living in this foreign land, but your country and your power to reign *is here in this land for now.*

Hear it again: Christians may be on earth physically, **but we are exalted; we sit in heaven with Jesus at the same time.** This is what it means to be exalted and when.

Part 2:20
The Keys of Authority

Satan has the power of death in his hands here on this earth. But Satan does not hold the power of death over the redeemed—**unless you allow him to have it.** You can allow him this power over your death by lacking the knowledge of your authority over the Devil **that belongs to you.**

God has allotted you your time on earth. You can let Satan change God's intention by not confronting the Devil. He can cause your early death either through sickness, an accident because you did not ask God for safety, or by sin that is blocking God's desires for you.

Never forget this is Satan's world. God has made a way out of this world while you are in it, **but it takes faith and trust to claim it.** Until you are willing to claim what is yours, you remain in Satan's world **under his control.**

The very words of Jesus found in John 10:10, make it clear Satan can take your life whenever he wants it. In the first chapter of Revelation, John wrote the words that he was given from Jesus Himself: *"Do not be afraid;* ¹⁸*I am the First and the Last. I am He who lives, and was dead, and behold, I am alive forevermore. Amen.* ***And I have the keys of Hades and of Death"*** (Revelation 1:17b, 18 NKJV).

Keys belong to those authorized to have them. When Adam sinned, Satan was then authorized to have the keys of death. Then Jesus arose and went to heaven. After His death He took back the keys for the part of mankind that are redeemed.

Those saints who trust in Jesus, also died with Jesus, and **they will not taste death again.** They have died with Christ and will transition from this wretched body to our new heavenly body.

> *"For we know that when this earthly tent we live in is taken down (that is, when we die and leave this earthly body), we will have a house in heaven and an eternal body made for us by God himself and not by human hands.*
>
> ²*We grow weary in our present bodies, and we long to put on our heavenly bodies like new clothing.* ³*For we will put on heavenly bodies;* ***we will not be spirits without bodies.***
>
> ⁴*While we live in these earthly bodies, we groan and sigh, but it's not that we want to die and get rid of these bodies that clothe us. Rather, we want to put on our new bodies so that these dying bodies will be swallowed up by life.*
>
> ⁵*God himself has prepared us for this, and as a guarantee He has given us his Holy Spirit"* (2 Corinthians 5:1-5 NLT).

Death is still an enemy **but only for the unbeliever.** The saints who die to Christ have died in the process of trusting Jesus. They will not die again. The reverse is true for those who do not love the Lord. They first die physically, then at the great white throne judgment they lose all hope. The Christian, on the other hand, dies eternally when he dies to Jesus; he simply changes location, as well as bodies.

These disclosures could be a new way of looking at knowledge found in the Bible for you. That certainly would be understandable as all of us carry religious baggage accumulated over the years.

Jesus promised that He would send the Holy Spirit to guide you in all truth. One way the Holy Spirit will guide you is through the Word of God, the Bible. Take these "new-to-you" Scriptures to the Lord and ask Him to give you a knowledge and an understanding of them. **That does not mean you can put the Book in a place of honor and just look at it. You must read it while asking God to direct His Holy Spirit to guide you into all truth.**

Part One of this book addressed the details of the Enemy, Satan.

Part Two addressed Who God is, what He has promised in relation to the Enemy, as well as how to increase your faith, and your God-given authority over the Evil One.

Part Three **will address more practical matters relating to spiritual warfare and how those in Jesus can defeat Satan and win victory.**

PART THREE

Father God, the Devil, and You

The Christian's Spiritual Warfare

The Christian's Spiritual Warfare

You have undoubtedly heard that if you begin reading a Scripture passage or even a book dealing with Scriptures with your mind already made up, your understanding is a foregone conclusion. However, *if you will begin by asking the Holy Spirit for understanding and enlightenment, you may learn something God wants you to know.*

Satan has a long history of creating doubt and unbelief with the use of half-truths, deception, and enticement. Early on, the book of Genesis discloses his first use of lies, deceit, and beguilement with something being withheld. Satan has never looked back since. He has only improved his tactics.

The ongoing battle between good and evil has really been a long running dispute between God and Satan with mankind in the middle. Humanity must make a choice if they wish to align themselves with God.

You can make it your choice or your choice will be made by default—especially if you prefer to align with the demonic realm. *If you choose to do nothing, you made your choice by default.*

To be included in God's kingdom, you must make a choice to accept the free gift that Jesus earned for you with His death on the cross. With that choice, your sins are gone. You will be the recipient of long-term beneficial rewards.

To be included in Satan's kingdom is easy, and that inclusion provides short-term pleasure right now, but long-term regrets later. Joining Satan's kingdom is easy because you don't have to do anything.

Your sinful human nature is already in alignment with the Devil's kingdom.

In his novel, *The Lord of the Flies*, William Golding penned, "Man produces evil as a bee produces honey." A quick review of the daily news confirms his observation.

The Christian who falls into Satan's trap should come as no real surprise. After all, Satan is the master of lies, deceit mixed with lies, and beguiling, or tempting the sinful human nature.

Personally, I doubt if a Christian can ever rise to the point in Christ when he or she will be completely immune to Satan's tactics.

When, **not if**, you fall or get caught in a sin, *ask the Lord for forgiveness, accept His forgiveness, and get up stronger in your faith and more aware of the Devil's tactics.*

Part 3:21
Your Authority Reviewed

Authority is "delegated power." What *power*?

Satan thought he had gotten rid of Jesus when he had Jesus nailed to the cross. God had a different plan, and He raised Jesus from the dead. Jesus then went to heaven; and from that time on, we never again read of Satan's being in heaven.

Jesus now reigns supreme in heaven, and the Scripture teaches that *Jesus is over all.*

When Jesus was raised to heaven, He went there as the head of the church. Jesus, the head of the church, remains in heaven, while the rest of His body—the redeemed Christians remain on earth.

Adam's sin gave this earth to Satan, and now Satan is on this earth full-time. The age-old battle between God and Satan continues, but their battle for the created beings known as man continues. **But that battle is no longer in both the heavenly and the earthly realms.**

Jesus said in Mark 29, that all authority has now been given to Him. **Jesus was now above the evil kingdom ruled by Satan.** Jesus is now in control over Satan and sits beside Father God, far above all powers and principalities.

In the tenth chapter of Luke, Jesus is recorded as first granting power over the Enemy to His 12 apostles and then to the 70 who were what I would consider as the lay people.

> *"I saw Satan falling from heaven as a flash of lightning! And I have given you authority over all the power of the Enemy, to walk among serpents and scorpions and to crush them"* (Luke 10:18b-19 TLB).

Even though Jesus had not yet been crucified and risen, this *authority* was His to grant. In effect, this authorization was only a foretaste of what was to come.

Therefore, the **power** spoken of in Mark 29 was power over Satan and his demonic realm. The word right before "power" is the word *authority*. God Himself delegated all power over Satan to Jesus. For that power to be further delegated, it would have to have been delegated by Jesus.

Part 3:22
Jesus Went to Heaven as Head of the Church

The rest of the church was obviously the body, and that part of His church consisted of the saints on earth. Therefore, the obvious answer as to who delegated the power to the body was Jesus. The obvious answer "to whom" was the church composed of a body of believers who were left behind to do a work, including defeating the schemes of the Devil and his cohorts. That work includes freedom from Satan's blocking or hindering our healing.

Therefore, if you are a child of Christ, you have authority over the Devil, and that includes all the power over him that Jesus has. In other words, you have the same power over Satan, *in the name of Jesus*, that Jesus has. You can exercise the authority of Jesus and be assured of His power to back up His authority.

However, the use of Jesus' name in either the demonic arena or in the arena of healing is **NOT** some "**magic** mantra" to be repeated to ward off evil, command the Devil to leave or to obtain our healing.

You must first grow your faith in Father God and in His Son Jesus Christ. Asking the Holy Spirit to give you the faith needed for believing what God has promised would also help. *Ask the Holy Spirit to provide the faith and assurance to you that Jesus has earned and won for you.*

Jesus provided for all the promises by leaving heaven, living here on earth, enduring beatings, being hung on a cross, and then trusting Father God to raise Him from the dead.

In his book entitled the Revelation, the apostle John added to the Christian's knowledge about Satan, our Enemy. The twelfth chapter of Revelation shares the account of Satan and his fallen angels being kicked out of heaven.

> *"And the great dragon was thrown down, that ancient serpent, who is called the devil and Satan, the deceiver of the whole world—he was thrown down to the earth, and his angels were thrown down with him.*

> ¹⁰*And I heard a loud voice in heaven, saying, 'Now the salvation and the power and the kingdom of our God and the authority of His Christ have come, for the accuser of our brothers has been thrown down, who accuses then day and night before our God.* ¹¹*And they have conquered him by the blood of the Lamb and by the word of their testimony, for they loved not their lives even unto death.* ¹²*Therefore, rejoice, O heavens and you who dwell in them! But woe to you, O earth and sea, for the devil has come down to you in great wrath, because he knows his time is short!"* (Revelation 12:9-12 ESV).

Just prior to this passage, Satan and his angels had fought with Michael and the angels of heaven, and they had been defeated. The resurrection of Jesus brought the death blow to the satanic realm. The battle has now moved from heaven to earth.

In the book of Revelation, John expanded on the passage found in the twelfth chapter. In the twentieth chapter, John wrote the following:

> *"Then I saw an angel coming down from heaven, holding in his hand the key to the bottomless pit and a great chain.* ²*And he seized the dragon, that ancient serpent, who is the devil and Satan, and bound him for a thousand years,* ³*and threw him into the pit, and shut it and sealed it over him, so that he might not deceive the nations any longer until the thousand years were ended. After that he must be released for a little while"* (Revelation 20:1-3 ESV).

In this interesting passage, the words *"a thousand years"* are not literal but a fullness of a time in God's eyes. Satan was only bound so that he could not deceive nations for that particular time period. However, He obviously is and has done a very credible job of deceiving the church during this time.

Part Three: The Christian's Spiritual Warfare

The angel went on to tell John that at the end of the fulfillment of that time, Satan would be released to deceive the nations once again—*but only for a little while.*

At this writing in the year 2022, when I look at the confusion in all the nations of this world, I must wonder if Satan has been released. What comes next? John's angel tells the reader in the next few verses:

> *"And when the thousand years are ended, Satan will be released from his prison and will come out to deceive the nations that are at the four corners of the earth, Gog and Magog, to gather them for battle; their number is like the sand of the sea.*
>
> *And they marched up over the broad plain of the earth and surrounded the camp of the saints and the beloved city, but fire came down from heaven and consumed them, and the devil who had deceived them was thrown into the lake of fire and sulfur where the beast and the false prophet were, and they will be tormented day and night forever and ever"* (Revelation 20:7-10 ESV).

Again the thousand years are a fulfillment of God's time—not a literal period of time. Gog and Magog could very well be God's realm and Satan's realm here on earth facing off for the end of the battle that began in heaven.

It is very unlikely that there will be a literal battle, as some teach. And the Bible is quite clear about where the Devil will be thrown, which is where the beast and the false prophet already are.

Faith for deliverance from the Enemy is the same faith the Holy Spirit gave us that enabled us to believe in what Jesus did for us to believe for our salvation.

Part 3:23
Your Authority Is Now

Paul wrote in Ephesians 1, *"Blessed be the God and Father of our Lord Jesus Christ, who hath blessed us with all spiritual blessings in heavenly places in Christ"* (v. 3 KJV).

Satanic authority belongs to you whether or not you realize it, but you must believe you have the authority to use it.

How tragic it is that the Western-world churches have allowed believers to go through their Christian life never knowing the power that is theirs with the phrase *"through Christ."* It is theirs, but they don't even know it! *Those blessings really belong to them.*

God's Word makes it clear that while we may be in this world, we are not of this satanic world. Satan does not have authority over us if we are a child of Christ—unless we want to give him that authority. Satan will do his best to convince us that he is in charge, but *unless we agree with him,* **Jesus is the only One in charge.**

Jesus died, came back to life, and ascended into heaven—**the victor over Satan.** God Himself delegated all authority both in heaven and on earth to Him.

Satan is no longer in heaven, so Jesus does not have to confront him there. Jesus is not physically on earth, so *He cannot confront the Devil here.* So, what did Jesus do? Jesus simply transferred His authority and power over Satan to His church. Our authority over the Enemy is NOW, and our NOW power is in the usage of Jesus' name.

Many Christians would like to leave everything to Jesus, especially where Satan and deliverance from his attacks are concerned.

Healing is the same. Many believers pray, "God heal me," *when, in God's eyes, He has already healed them through what Jesus Christ endured for their health and healing with the stripes He bore on His back.*

Jesus died for our sins, and all we have to do is to believe by faith that He did so. Jesus rose from the dead, and in the process, He defeated Satan and his followers. All we have to do to enjoy the fruits of what He has done for us is to believe by faith. His victory is ours to use against Satan.

Because sickness and disease are often addressed together, I will remind you that the prophet Isaiah said Jesus suffered the stripes being lashed on His back so man could enjoy healing. The authority over the demonic realm is yours, **but only if you are willing to claim it by faith.** The stripes Jesus bore on His back at Calvary paid the price for your healings, **but only if you will claim it by faith.**

Many problems exist in your life as a Christian because you permit them to. You have the authority because Jesus Christ delegated it to you. **You are now the one who is supposed to do something about the Devil and his followers.**

Part 3:24
Reigning as Kings

Paul wrote in Ephesians,

"Even when we were dead in trespasses, [GOD] *made us alive together with Christ (by grace you have been saved), ⁶and raised us up together, and made us sit together in the heavenly places in Christ Jesus"* (Ephesians 2:5-6 NKJV).

Jesus is in heaven; Paul is here writing to the church at Ephesus. Obviously, Paul was living when he wrote this letter, and the saints at

Ephesus were also living. God said that they were alive with Christ with Jesus.

Once a person is born again, biblically it seems that spiritually we are living in heaven with Jesus. Even though physically our bodies are still here on earth.

I like the way this same passage reads in The Living Bible translation as follows:

> *"But God is so rich in mercy; he loved us so much ⁵that even though we were spiritually dead and doomed by our sins, he gave us back our lives again when he raised Christ from the dead— only by his undeserved favor have we ever been saved—⁶and [He] lifted us up from the grave into glory along with Christ, where we sit with him in the heavenly realms—all because of what Christ Jesus did"* (Ephesians 2:4-6 TLB).

The reader will notice the passage has been made more personable by changing the pronoun **"we"** to **"you."**

Jesus is now in heaven where He is reigning. **Kings reign!**

The same God Who raised up Jesus to reign in heaven saved you and me who were not deserving of being saved. **But God did not stop there.** At the same time God raised Christ to a reigning position in heaven, He raised you and me to heaven as well.

Jesus Christ reigns, and we reign with Him. **Kings reign, Jesus reigns, you and I reign with Him.** *The Word says that we, though alive on this earth, are in reality reigning with Him in heaven.*

In Romans 5, Paul makes it clear that if you are in Christ Jesus, then even as He reigns as King, we are reigning with Him. We may not know all there is to know about reigning with Him but take it at face value and don't try to question it.

I have already stated that when God says something, even though in actuality what He said will be made evident at a later time, *in His eyes it as if it were already accomplished.*

Part 3:25
Temptation: From Where Does It Come?

The prayer the Jesus taught His disciples at their request contained an interesting bit of verbiage: *"And lead us not into temptation, but deliver us from evil..."* (Matthew 6:13 KJV).

Jesus is teaching a prayer to Father God for His disciples, so when He says **not** to lead us into temptation, He is asking God **not** to lead them into any temptation, **not** to deliver them from the temptation.

If God is being asked **not** to lead us into any temptations, that leaves only one possibility; Satan and his evil followers will lead us into temptation! The Devil will lead you into temptation, and he will try to partner with you to sin. However, **you can partner with God to keep you from that temptation!**

The Devil works with your sinful nature not only to lead you into temptation, but he will do everything possible to get you to act on that temptation. Satan will lead directly, his fallen angels will lead directly, and either or both will also use other humans to lead you into temptation. Your battle is a daily combat with the Devil, whether he comes directly, sends a demon, or uses a "demon-led" person to hide the real culprit. *And that battle continues whether or not you acknowledge it is possible.*

> *"For we are not fighting against people made of flesh and blood, but against persons without bodies—the evil rulers of the unseen world, those mighty satanic beings and great evil prince of dark-*

ness who rule this world; and against huge numbers of wicked spirits in the spirit world" (Ephesians 6:12 TLB).

Two points of note regarding this biblical passage: Paul is making it quite clear that simply because we have accepted Christ as our Savior will not make the Devil throw up a white flag of surrender and not bother us. *Not only has the fight continued on earth after Satan was thrown out of heaven, but Paul makes it very clear exactly how organized Satan is.*

The other observation from this passage makes the organization of Satan's kingdom abundantly clear. *The number of evil deities is huge.* Maybe a demon isn't hiding behind every bush, but I am wagering one might be hiding behind every bush shielding a Christian.

Human events that occur in your life, especially events that affect you personally such as sickness, disease, death, accidents, family relationships involving marriage and children, are often put under additional pressure, or made worse by demonic involvement.

Anything of importance to a child of God faces spiritual involvement. If you confront a negative situation, the Devil will use your weak immune system at that time to move in and wreak havoc. If you let him, believe me, the bad situation will become exponentially worse.

Thankfully, the apostle Paul in Ephesians and Solomon in Proverbs furnish the Christian with an out. Solomon wrote the following in Proverbs:

> *"Do not be afraid of sudden terror, nor of trouble from the wicked when it comes; [26]for the* Lord *will be your confidence, and will keep you from being caught"* (Proverbs 3:25-26 NKJV).

Proverbs, of course, was written before Jesus defeated Satan with His resurrection. Now, in addition to the confidence we can have in Father

God, we have the authority over Satan through Jesus' victory over him. Plus, you have the power of Jesus' name to seal the deal.

A spiritual world surrounds us whether or not we know it. **All our denials or ignorance of this world will not change reality.** The spirit world consists of both God and Satan as the leaders of their realms. The rest of Matthew 6:13, *"deliver us from evil,"* should probably include the words: "and the evil ones." The words "deliver us from evil" is the direct opposite of the partnership between the Devil and your sinful nature.

Now Father God, through what Jesus has accomplished in the defeat of the Devil, *partners with the Holy Spirit and you to grant you the power to deliver you from the temptation of the Devil.* Through the power of the Holy Spirit, you can recognize the temptation for what it is. Then you can use the power that is yours through Jesus Christ's name to command that temptation to leave…**and it will.**

In John 10:10 Jesus forthrightly tells all of us exactly what Satan has come to do—first in heaven and earth—and now only on earth. *"The thief comes only to steal and kill and destroy…"* (John 10:10 ESV).

Previously I addressed what Jesus meant with the words *"steal, kill, and destroy."* They mean exactly what you would think they mean in your worst possible thoughts.

The good news from Jesus is the rest of the verse where Jesus added the following words: *"I came that they may have life and have it abundantly."*

What Jesus has made available for the saints, both here on the earth and then for all eternity, is abundantly clear. **How do you understand the words of Jesus when He said** *abundantly***?**

Again, though, the decision as to which choice you will make is yours to make. The Devil wants your partnership, and so does your

Heavenly Father. The difference is the Devil will not forgive you of your sins and will do everything he can to keep you; *while God will forgive you and welcome you back.*

Even if a person is filled with the Holy Spirit, the devil will not go away or leave that person alone. **I can hear you say, "Oh, no, that can't be!"** Unless the stories I read in my Bible are incorrect, then all of us are susceptible to the demonic beings.

Even after being filled with the Holy Spirit in the upper room, the leaders of the early church still had to deal with the demonic forces. The writers of many of the New Testament books of the Bible mentioned that fact often. But let's not stop with the early church leaders. Jesus had been filled with the Holy Spirit at His baptism when he was led into the wilderness.

That filling of the Holy Spirit did not keep the Devil from attacking Jesus with various temptations. The fact that Jesus was "filled" with the Spirit did not make Him immune. And even when Jesus ordered the Devil to "get away," and he did, that order did not stop the Devil from returning and trying again.

Some translations read the Devil departed *until a more opportune time*. Take my word of experience. You may defeat the Devil, but that defeat will not keep him from coming back. The sad part of his coming back repeatedly is that you will not always see him coming. Satan can already have you in a bad place before the Holy Spirit makes you aware of what he has done or how he got back in. **What do you do when that occurs?**

Ask God to forgive you for being snookered. Remember Who has the authority over the Evil One. Also remember Who has invested His authority over the demonic realm in *you*. **You order that foul spirit out of you in the power of Jesus' name.**

Trust me, he will have to go. Also use the Word of God as a sword both to fight the Devil and to defeat him when he attacks you or your family.

Part 3:26
Free Will Always Prevails

Jesus made it clear in Luke regarding your authority concerning the Devil. Your authority over the demonic realm can play a huge role in how your free will works out in your day-to-day living.

"Behold, I give you authority to trample on serpents and scorpions, and over all the power of the enemy, and nothing shall by any means hurt you" (Luke 10:19 NKJV).

Temptation comes from the Devil, and sometimes God will allow the temptation to see how you will react to it. However, if you want to fight against temptation, Jesus through His victory over the Devil will provide you with His power to resist and to defeat the Enemy.

He will also provide you with the authority to trample him. *With that authority, you can command the Devil to leave,* and "in the name and power of Jesus," he will have to leave.

Jesus finalized His words found in Luke regarding the total defeat of the Devil. Satan had been removed from heaven, and now Paul, under the inspirational of the Holy Spirit, states it this way:

"I pray that you will begin to understand how incredibly great His power is to help those who believe him. It is the same mighty power [20]that raised Christ from the dead and seated him in the place of honor at God's right hand in heaven, [21]far, far above any other king or ruler or dictator or leader. Yes, his honor is

far more glorious than that of anyone else in this world or in the world to come. ²²And God has put all things under his feet and made him the supreme Head of the Church—²³which is his body, filled with Himself..." (Ephesians 1:19-23 TLB).

Paul realizes just how great God's power is, and he is trying to help his readers catch what he understands about God's power.

Why God allowed Satan to remain in heaven for as long as He did, we will probably never know. But now, according to the book of Revelation, all evil and rebellion has been removed from heaven. Only *the angels and the redeemed saints who have died remain in heaven.*

God has placed Jesus at His right hand, and He has put all things both in heaven and on earth under His control. *Paul makes it very clear that Jesus is the Head of His church, and Jesus then filled the church with Himself.* That fact should make it very clear from where our authority and power over the demonic realm comes. And as Head of His church, if you are in Christ, His authority and power are yours to use over the Devil. *But here is where the rubber meets the road!* The choice of whether or not to avail yourself of the gift He has made available to you is yours to make.

Question: *do you want to call God a liar? Are you willing to slap Jesus in the face and tell Him you don't think the price He paid on your behalf is equal to Satan's lies?*

The cost that Jesus paid at Calvary was great; **your cost is non-existent.** The only bump in the road is that **you must make the choice** between what God has made available and what Satan promises you. Satan however, is a liar in what he promises. **God does not lie.**

God made free will a choice in heaven, and God has made free will a choice on earth as well.

Part 3:27
It Always Comes Down to Your Choice

The Bible has made it clear that Jesus has defeated the Devil, and He has been elevated far above Satan and all his hierarchy. Satan would like to lie to you and convince you that he is equal to God, or at least Jesus, **but he is not.**

The battle in your mind regarding God or the Devil's kingship continues while the choice of which entity you will serve remains yours.

Part 3:28
Satanic Oppression or Possession?

Whether a Christian can be oppressed or possessed has long been a question. Theologians have long argued this question. I have reviewed both sides of this theological question and will share with you my thoughts, but on this one you will need to make up your own mind.

Before the coming of Jesus to this earth, when people were not themselves, they were said to be possessed with a foul spirit. After Jesus came, people began to learn the difference between a person's being sold out to Satan or a person's being influenced by the evil realm. A person could be a believer in Christ and still be afflicted and tormented by Satan. A Christian can be even controlled by the Enemy **but not possessed.**

If you owned a large house, Satan could be in a room or several rooms, and Jesus could be in a room or several rooms at the same time. You own the house, and you make the choice of being willing to have mixed renters. You make the decision as to whether you want occupancy by the Devil alone, or Jesus alone, or **both having occupancy**

in your home. Even Christians will have a difficult time keeping out the Devil, *or if it comes to that,* **kicking him out.**

This is your choice, but keep in mind, if you willingly allow Satan *in your home, it will be easier for him to control your sinful thoughts. If you decide later that you don't want him in your home, it will be harder for you to remove him.* **In my opinion this situation describes** *oppression*—not *possession.*

I personally believe there are levels of oppression that can trouble the Christian, but possession can never take place in a Christian's life. *Why do I say that?* In the life of a child of God, the Holy Spirit indwells that person at the time he accepts Jesus as his Savior. Until the individual basically chooses to have the Holy Spirit leave and invites Satan to take over, it is oppression.

Part 3:29
Christians Can Only be Oppressed

The Christian can be oppressed from the inside out or from the outside *in.*

I believe Satan is just as willing to oppress an unbeliever as he is when he tries to oppress the believer. He will oppress both *because that is what he attempts to do to everyone!* It is easier for Satan to get the unbeliever to cross over into an evil life where Satan has complete control. **At that point, a person becomes** *possessed.*

Let me use a couple of biblical illustrations. John tells the story of Judas at the Last Supper: *"During supper, when the devil had already put it into the heart of Judas Iscariot, Simon's son to betray Him"* (John 13:2 ESV).

The thought in Judas' mind started way before the supper, but at

Part Three: The Christian's Spiritual Warfare

the supper Judas let Satan have complete control. And as a famous radio announcer always said, *"Now you know the rest of the story...."*

I am reminded of the story of the temptation of Jesus shortly after He had been filled with the Holy Spirit at His baptism. *In this case Satan put the thoughts into Jesus' mind with his questions and promises, but Jesus never let the thoughts progress.* And even after Satan left Him, some translations read that Satan only left until another more opportune time presented itself.

Even with Jesus, Satan never gave up.

Another example is Ananias and his wife Sapphira, who were thought to be believers. Satan injected the plan into their minds to keep back part of the money they had promised God from the sale of an asset. Peter said to Ananias, *"Why has Satan filled your heart to lie to the Holy Spirit?"* (Acts 5:3 ESV). At this point, the oppression of a thought changed to one of possession.

Luke 13 includes the story of a daughter of Abraham who had been oppressed by Satan for 18 years. Jesus did not say she was possessed, only oppressed. The Bible includes other stories such as Peter's mother-in-law having a spirit of fever or of being oppressed by a spirit.

After the ascension of Jesus, in the tenth chapter of Acts, Peter said, *"God anointed Jesus of Nazareth with the Holy Spirit and with power. He went about doing good and healing all who were oppressed by the devil, for God was with him"* (Acts 10:38 ESV).

I realize we have been discussing the difference between oppression and possession in the life of a Christian, but this verse not only deals with the subject but adds another dimension to the subject of deliverance.

I have often found in my life that healing and deliverance go together. When I have claimed healing that is promised by the stripes

Jesus bore on His back, many times I have also had to command the Devil to get out before I can realize my God-given healing.

I honestly do not know if my healing comes because of the stripes that Jesus bore on His back, or if somehow Satan got to where he could oppress me in the that sickness.

The writer of the book of Acts made an interesting observation when he wrote the following in the fifth chapter:

> *"And believers were increasingly added to the Lord, multitudes of both men and women, ¹⁵so that they brought the sick out into the streets and laid them on beds and couches, that at least the shadow of Peter passing might fall on them. ¹⁶Also a multitude gathered from the surrounding cities to Jerusalem, **bringing sick people and those who were tormented by unclean spirits, and they were healed"*** (Acts 5:14-16 NKJV).

The writer makes it clear that sickness can be caused by demonic activity. The question is whether the healings happened due to casting out the demons *or were they healed because of the stripes that Jesus bore on His back when He restored healing to His created beings? Or could the healing have been a combination of both?* My personal experiences would suggest that often it takes faith in both functions to be healed.

There have been other occasions where I have let in the Devil for whatever reason. Before I could be healed because of the stripes that Jesus endured on His back, I had to use my God-given authority over Satan and command the Devil to leave. If sin was involved, I would need to confess that sin and ask God to forgive me. **Father God has never refused to forgive me, and then healing was the result.** It seems that far too often the demonic had moved in during a sickness, and all three actions were required.

Part Three: The Christian's Spiritual Warfare

An interesting passage found in Luke 4 says that the Devil sometimes works from the inside and oppresses people, and sometimes Jesus worked with people Satan was attacking from the outside when oppressing them.

Whether the Devil gets on the inside because of **sickness, diseases, depression,** or *is allowed in because of unforgiven sins, anger, lust, shame, fear, or hatred*, the result is the same. The Christian suffers, and the Devil needs to be dealt with. Repent or ask forgiveness if needed. Then rebuke the Devil specifically by naming the intrusion. *Then take the authority that Jesus has made available and command that demonic entity to get out in Jesus' name.*

As Kenneth Hagin said in *The Believer's Authority*, the demon will not only have to go, but he will flee from you at the name of Jesus.

Jesus made it very clear where His followers are to take the message of authority over the demonic. Jesus words in Matthew 10 are very suggestive:

> *"Go rather to the lost sheep of Israel. As you go, proclaim this message: 'The kingdom of heaven has come near.' Heal the sick, raise those who have leprosy,* **drive out demons.** *Freely you have received, freely give"* (Matthew 10:7-8 NIV).

Just as Israel was considered the lost sheep of that day, so are the Christians of this day.

This message of deliverance from the satanic realm should first be taught in the church. *The pastors, church leaders, teachers, and even the believers who have the faith in today's world need to be the ones taking the message to the local church that obviously has the need to know.*

The local church needs to be taught to believe what Jesus has made available and how to appropriate what is theirs to use and/or receive. I have read my Bible from cover to cover many times, and I have never found where the power over the Devil has ever been rescinded. Nor for that matter did I ever find where the power of Jesus to heal has ever been removed either.

Part 3:30
Satan and His Followers Are Active Everywhere

The first instance of Satan's operating inside the body of an animal is found in the garden of Eden. Satan had invaded a snake or a scorpion to gain a dialogue with Eve. Satan is referred to as *"a roaring lion"* (I Peter 5:8), or a fearsome creature taken over by demons.

Matthew 8 includes the story of a multitude of demons being allowed to go into a drove of pigs, and those demons caused the pigs to jump into the sea and drown.

Many stories are told of animals such as dogs or wild animals that act demonic at times. So yes, I believe demons can invade animals.

What about nature? Can the demonic take control of nature? I address only one incident in the Bible. When the disciples were crossing the Sea of Galilee, and a merciless storm blew in. *If this had been only an event of nature, Jesus would not have rebuked the storm, commanding the storm to be still.* I think it is safe to conclude that Satan wanted to take Jesus and His disciples out in this storm.

Multitudes of stories are posted on the Internet of saints commanding storms to be still and of hurricanes directed to detour around certain places. The list is endless. Indeed, Satan will use natural events, but God is in control of nature. Satan will use natural causes to cause trouble for mankind, and God will use natural events to test, punish, lead, or direct mankind.

PART THREE: THE CHRISTIAN'S SPIRITUAL WARFARE

The bottom line is: God is in control all the time!

Part 3:31
Satanic Preparation, Now and for Eternity

God allowed Lucifer free will in heaven. Satan could have chosen to give obedience to God, as God intended. But Satan allowed his pride to control him and instead challenged God's authority. God said He created humanity just a little lower than the angels *for a time.*

I read somewhere that Satan would rather reign in hell than serve in Heaven. What a shame! **Satan could not allow mere humans to rise to a level above his exalted status, so he challenged God's authority.**

Satan, of course, lost his challenge to God's authority, but for whatever reason, it seems that God allowed Satan to dwell in heaven for a time. At the same time, God allowed Satan to continue to seduce the descendants of Adam and Eve to sin. Except for Israel, God allowed the nations of the world to be seduced by Satan for a long time.

The nation of Israel was protected from being deceived by Satan. However, the children of God, both then and now, have done a good job of sinning against God without Satan's specific help.

After Jesus came to earth, John wrote that Satan was being chained so that he could no longer deceive nations for a specific time. The church, Christ's body, then took over as God's favorite "people."

As the church, God's favorite people are having as much trouble living the life that God intended as did the Israelites. **God is using Satan and this present world as a testing ground for the redeemed who will live with Him for eternity in heaven.**

Under the inspirational of the Holy Spirit, Paul phrased this so well in the second chapter of Colossians.

> *"He [God] took this list of sins and destroyed it by nailing it to Christ's cross. ¹⁵In this way God took away Satan's power to accuse you of sin, and God openly displayed to the whole world Christ's triumph at the cross where your sins were all taken away"* (Colossians 2:14-15 TLB).

God may use Satan and his evil realm to test you and to prepare you for heaven. The Devil and all his host were not only defeated by Jesus Christ, but they were also thrown out of heaven.

Satan is no longer able to accuse you before God in heaven. God still allows the Devil to entice you not only to sin but also for you to give your allegiance to him.

The battle goes on and will continue to go on until the end of this earth, but the war is won. *The testing ground for your loyalty to God takes place before you get to heaven.*

God will allow Satan to test you, and to place temptations before you. Satan will lie to you, and he will promise you whatever it takes to draw you away from God.

God has given you His plan to overcome the Devil when he attacks you in whatever way. However, faith in Jesus Christ is the authority and power God provided you to overcome the Devil.

It shouldn't take a rocket scientist to observe that Christians within the body of Christ are failing miserably. In my book entitled, *Heaven, Expect the Unexpected*, I shared the stories of many Christians who had died, gone to heaven, and came back.

Those "Near-Death Experiencers" (NDErs) told how Jesus had conducted a "life review" before sending the Christian back. In these reviews, Jesus asked the following question of each one: **"What have you done for Me with the life that I have given you?"**

Part Three: The Christian's Spiritual Warfare

The answer Jesus was hoping to hear was not the answer the NDErs gave. *Whether you can believe that saints have died, gone to heaven, and returned is immaterial. Indeed, every saint should ask and answer this question.*

Serving on the church board, feeding the hungry, teaching Sunday school class, preaching, etc. all missed what Jesus wanted from His redeemed souls.

Enoch, as well as other Old Testament figures, plus Paul and John are all Biblical figures who went to heaven and returned.

How would you answer Jesus if He asked you the question, "What have you done with the life I gave you?"

After they had experienced a near-death experience, the NDErs were returned to life on this earth. Each reported how his or her life was changed.

I have digressed. God wants to make sure you will remain loyal to Him once He allows you into His heaven. Yes, I think the Book is clear that you will have your free will in heaven. Why would God want robots in heaven? Plus, God has already set the precedent with Satan and the fallen angels. If any of God's created beings should not have been expected to have a free will, I would not have thought God would allow the angels that option.

Part 3:32
In It to Win It

Among his other faults, Satan will try to hinder you in performing God's will in your life.

Paul a devout servant of God, and concerned to be doing God's will, wrote in the book of Thessalonians just how effective Satan is in hindering a Christian from doing God's will in their life. *"Therefore, we wanted to come to you—even I, Paul, time and again—**but Satan hindered us**"* (1 Thessalonians 2:18 NKJV).

We do not know why didn't Satan want Paul to go to the saints at Thessalonica. We only know he did not want Paul to go at that time. The Bible contains many other instances where Satan hindered the work of God.

Satan hinders the work of God in another way that is even more insidious. I believe Paul's warning to the church at Corinth is a warning for today believers: *"The kingdom of God is not just talking: it is living by God's power"* (1 Corinthians 4:20 TLB). Paul added to this warning when he wrote the following to Timothy in his second letter: *"Having a form of godliness, but denying its power"* (3:5).

In today's terminology, Paul would be telling Timothy that people who attend church to look good and to do good on their own could be fooling themselves. Doing good in the ways Jesus Christ demonstrated requires doing good in His power. To do good in the ways Jesus taught and did involves faith to use the power He has made available.

Part 3:33
Most of Today's Christians Deny that Power Is Part of the Faith

James, the brother of Jesus, wrote to address a problem that was creeping into the church of that day. The church may have addressed the problem then, but it seems to have resurfaced today.

*"But be doers of the word, and not hearers only, **deceiving yourselves**"* (James 1:22 NKJV).

James is telling his listeners if they were not doing the last words of Jesus found in Matthew and Mark given to them at His ascension, they were basically kidding themselves.

Paul wrote to Timothy, his *"son in the faith"* shortly before he knew his death was imminent. Paul knew that the last days of the Jewish religion, the Jewish life, and the Jewish temple were soon to come, and the life they had known would all change.

Granted, Paul thought Jesus was coming back, and that would be the end of time. Paul did not know the exact details, but he knew enough. Jesus did come back in AD 70, and that was the end of things for the Jews of that time.

Jesus came in judgment for the Jews—not for the entire world. Jesus came on the clouds of judgment, **but the judgment was selective at that coming.**

The warning Paul passed on to Timothy for the Christian of that day should be heeded in today's church age as well.

> *"You may as well know this too, Timothy, that in the last days it is going to be very difficult to be a Christian. ²For people will love only themselves and their money; they will be proud and boastful, sneering at God, disobedient to their parents, ungrateful to them, and thoroughly bad. ³They will be hardheaded and never give in to others; they will be constant liars and troublemakers and will think nothing of immorality. They will be rough and cruel, and sneer at those who try to be good. ⁴They will betray their friends; they will be hotheaded, puffed up with pride, and prefer good times to worshipping God. ⁵****They will go to church, yes, but they won't really believe anything they hear...****"* (2 Timothy 3:1-5 TLB).

Paul did not know he was speaking about the end of the Jewish age—*not the end of the world*. But Paul saw what was taking place in the lives of the Christians of that day. Now, over 2000 years later, the warning Paul passed on to Timothy should be heeded in today's church age.

Take a few minutes to go through the list and see if you don't identify with Paul's warning to Timothy and compare it to what is happening in America today.

The fight about which Paul warned so many years ago has now changed. Paul summed up the fight against Satan and his wicked followers; and that fight continues today.

> *"Finally, my brethren, be strong in the Lord and in the power of His might. [You] ¹¹put on the whole armor of God, that you may be able to stand against the wiles of the devil. ¹²For we do not wrestle against flesh and blood, but against principalities, against powers, against the rulers of the darkness of this age, against spiritual hosts of wickedness in the heavenly places. ¹³Therefore take up the whole armor of God, that you may be able to withstand in the evil day, having done all, to stand"* (Ephesians 6:10-13 NKJV).

Paul is now near the end of his earthly journey; God has told Paul that he is coming home. Paul warns the believers he will be leaving behind that until Jesus comes back for the final time, the fight with the Devil will continue.

In this passage Paul wants the Christians to know that the Enemy is formidable and very well organized. He ends the warning with a passage telling the believer what armor to wear and how to fight.

Paul goes on in the next passage to tell the armor needed to resist and to defeat the Enemy:

Part Three: The Christian's Spiritual Warfare

"[You] Stand therefore, having girded your waist with truth, having put on the breastplate of righteousness, ¹⁵and having shod your feet with the preparation of the gospel of peace; ¹⁶above all, taking the shield of faith with which you will be able to quench all the fiery darts of the wicked one. ¹⁷And take the helmet of salvation, and the sword of the Spirit, which is the word of God; ¹⁸praying always with all prayer and supplication in the Spirit, being watchful to this end with all perseverance and supplication for all the saints" (Ephesians 6:14-18 NKJV).

The conventional armor that Paul listed was the best armor available in those days. The traveler in those days wore long robes, and they had a belt around their waist where they tucked in the bottom of the robe so they would not trip.

If your belt is the belt of truth found in God's Word, you will not find yourself tripped up in your walk with the lies of Satan.

Temptation always start in the mind. You can get rid of the potential sin at that point, or if you keep thinking on the sin, it will travel into your heart. Paul told his readers to put on the breastplate of righteousness. **If you do that the sin that is trying to tempt, you will not get into your heart.**

Paul goes on to say, walk in the shoes of peace; and don't forget the shield of faith. **Faith will defeat the lies (the fiery darts) of the Devil every time.** Remember faith is the same as trust, and God doesn't lie, **so you can trust Him.**

God remembers to protect your mind, which is the reason for the helmet. Satan will try to convince you the promises of God are not what you think, which is why you need protection for your head and mind.

Okay, God has done everything He can to protect you. Now it is your turn to fight. The sword of the Spirit is the Word of God in your mouth, empowered by the enlightenment of the Holy Spirit, and backed up with the power that Jesus has made available. Step up to the plate and take on the Enemy. Pray the words found in the Bible. Throw them at the Enemy as you would throw a knife if you were in a fight.

Trust me, the words of the Lord will hit the target every time!

Paul added to the weapons of our satanic warfare against Satan in the second book of Corinthians. Paul writes that, in his human condition, he would lose the battle:

"It is true that I am an ordinary, weak human being, but I don't use human plans and methods to win my battles. ⁴I use God's mighty weapons, not those made by men, to knock down the devil's strongholds" (2 Corinthians 10:3-4 TLB).

You and I are no stronger than Paul, so what are these mighty weapons Paul is using? You will notice where the weapons Paul is using are in the following passage:

"Casting down arguments and every high thing that exalts itself against the knowledge of God, bring every thought into captivity to the obedience of Christ" (2 Corinthians 10:5 TLB).

Paul knows where the Devil has access to you and where you are the most vulnerable. **That weak point is your mind.** *All temptation, as well as the decision to sin, not only originates in your mind, but when you lose the inward fight against that temptation, it leaves the mind and moves into your very being—the heart.* Paul doesn't quit with the words found in Ephesians. Paul goes on the say that God Himself has a vested interest in the battle between Himself and Satan. *"He* [God] *has delivered us from the power of darkness and conveyed us into the kingdom of the Son of His love"* (Colossians 1:13 NKJV).

God has taken the Christian from under the power of Satan, which Paul calls darkness. God not only gave the Christian a way out of Satan's darkness, but then God took us to heaven—even while we reside here on earth. *Why did He do that?*

Jesus as head of the church is seated in heaven far above Satan and his powers. **God seated us in heaven with Christ so that we may know that we are also seated above the evil kingdom of the Devil.**

Jesus is reigning now, and we reign with Him.

PART FOUR

Father God, the Devil, and You

Your Victory Over Satan Begins NOW

Your Victory Over Satan Begins NOW

Part 4:34
Your Authority Review

Any Christian's authority, including yours, comes originally from Father God Himself. God is the One Who delegated His authority to Jesus Christ. That total delegated power included power over all the heavenly created angels, as well as all created humans here on earth.

Originally when Lucifer, or Satan, was created, it appears that Lucifer was created as the head angel. That changed when Jesus rose from the dead and ascended into heaven. **Jesus then had total control over Satan and all his fallen angels.** Part II determined our source to support that God has the ultimate authority, which He delegated to Jesus Christ, was from the Bible.

Following Jesus' ascension into heaven, Satan and his followers were driven out of heaven. Part II also addressed the authority that had been delegated to Jesus was then delegated to the true church, which now has authority over Satan and his evil realm. In addition to the authority Jesus passed on to His followers, He backed up this authority with His power. When Jesus gave His authority to the church, you then being seated with Christ in heaven, were indued with Jesus' authority and with His power.

According to the Word, God sees the Christian as being seated in heaven with Jesus Christ NOW. *As far as God or Jesus are concerned, your power over Satan is NOW while you are here on this earth.*

PART FOUR: YOUR VICTORY OVER SATAN BEGINS NOW

A word of caution: you will have absolutely no power over Satan in your life if you do not know the Word or are not willing to trust Jesus in more than just paying the price for your sins. You may be saved eternally, but your earthly walk is based on your understanding of the Word and the Holy Spirit within you.

Remember, faith—even your faith to believe Jesus died for your sins—comes by hearing the Word of God found in the Bible. *Without faith, which is no more than trust in God, His Son, and enhanced by His Spirit, you have no chance of defeating the Devil in the daily activities of your life.*

Part 4:35
Remembering Where You Are

The bottom line is that the Christian is now in heaven ruling with Jesus, even while living on earth. In the second chapter of Ephesians, the apostle Paul said it so well:

"Even when we were dead in trespasses, [God] made us alive together with Christ (by grace you have been saved), ⁶and raised us up together, and made us sit together in heavenly places in Christ Jesus" (vv. 5-6 NKJV).

*"But God is so rich in mercy; he loved **you** so much ⁵that even though **you** were spiritually dead and doomed by **your** sins, he gave us back our lives again when he raised Christ from the dead—only by his undeserved favor have **you** ever been saved— ⁶and [God] lifted **you** up from the grave into glory along with Christ, where **you** sit with him in the heavenly realms—all because of what Christ Jesus did"* (vv. 4-6 TLB; emphasis mine).

Once again, I have changed the pronoun *we* to *you* (in bold) for personalization. Paul wrote these words to the Ephesians while he (and they) were still living on earth. Clearly, in God's mindset, He sees believers as being in heaven right now. If you are born again, you may still be physically on earth, but spiritually you are already in heaven sitting with Jesus Christ.

Jesus is now in heaven where He is sitting and reigning with God. This is the same God Who raised Jesus from the dead. Jesus now reigns from heaven over all, including the Devil and his realm of fallen angels. We are in heaven right now reigning with Jesus. That being the case, we, the church, even though physically on earth, are reigning over the Devil and all his fallen angels.

Part 4:36
Faith Review

The authority over the demonic realm is ours, but only if we are willing to claim it by faith. We must trust Jesus enough to use the authority He has delegated to us and have faith in His promise to back up the authority with the power available to us through use of His name.

Many problems exist in the life of a Christian simply because the Christian allows them. This suffering can be because of the lack of knowledge, or the problems can exist because the Christian isn't willing to trust Jesus of being capable to provide what He has promised.

How a Christian can muster up enough faith to believe Jesus in His promise of eternal life in heaven with Father God and His Son but can't find enough faith to trust Him for all the promises that Jesus and His Father have made available for the duration of his life while here on earth is strange, for lack of a better word.

The faith for us to believe Jesus for the forgiveness of our sins and the promise of eternal life needs faith supplied to us by the Holy Spirit. Please ask the Holy Spirit to give you the faith to believe in your authority over the Devil, and while you are asking, why don't you ask Him for the faith to believe Jesus for the healing He has promised as well?

Jesus said it so well when He said in the gospel of John how we can expect to learn all things: directly from the Bible, from the pulpit, or from a book like this one.

"But the Counselor, the Holy Spirit, whom the Father will send in My name, He will teach you all things, and bring to your remembrance all things that I said to you" (John 14:26 RSV).

The Bible says that God will never give a stone when He is asked for bread. You ask, and He will give; *you only have to trust Him. Trust me, He is trustworthy.*

Part 4:37
Who Are You Fighting?

By now it should be obvious that the Christian is fighting God's Enemy, the Devil. Lucifer was originally created perfect, and he was given a very exalted position in heaven—probably the highest position in heaven beneath the Trinity.

The Bible indicates that Satan learned God intended His new creation would one day be exalted higher than the angels, which also included him. **Satan's pride could not handle that knowledge.** The sin of pride was the root cause of his rebellion against God.

As a side note: *I would suspect that Satan used God's intention of* *raising humans above the angels as a tool to persuade the other angels to join his rebellion.*

We have no idea how much time passed between the moment Satan learned of God's intention to elevate man and when biblical history records that Satan caused Adam and Eve to sin in the garden. We do know their sin caused the fall of humanity and passed rulership of the earth to Satan.

Now instead of having Satan alone to fight, mankind also had his rotten and corrupt nature joining the fight against God.

The question is: **who are we fighting?**

God and Satan are in a war, with humans as the prize. God has already defeated and kicked Satan and his angels out of heaven. The war has now been removed to earth. Satan wants you to join his evil realm, and if you do, you will have eternity to be with him in hell. ***But if you chose God as your partner and are willing to accept His offer to forgive all your sins through Jesus Christ, you will receive His promise of eternal life in heaven with Him.***

Satan will offer his angels to help you get what you think you want on this earth. They will lie, cheat, entice, beguile, promise, deceive, or anything else needed to get what the evil realm wants. God, on the other hand, offers the Holy Spirit and the power of His Son to get all that He has promised to you—both in this life and in the one to come.

You are the prize in the fight between God and Satan. The war is already won, and Satan knows who the winner is. Satan could not defeat Jesus with His death on the cross. When God raised Jesus back to life, Jesus instead then defeated Satan with His resurrection from death. Following Jesus' ascension to heaven, God finally threw Satan and his rebellious angels out of heaven.

At that point, the war was over in heaven between God and Satan.

However, God only wants humans in heaven who want Him and will be loyal to Him. So, the battle for that loyalty continues between God and Satan here on earth. The battles continue for all on a day-to-day basis until you die, and then your part of the battle is over. The choices you made while you were still breathing will determine who gets the prize.

The bottom line is that the fight is a complicated one. After researching material for this book for the past 24 months, my thought is that God planned it this way so earth can not only be a training ground for Christians prior to heaven, but earth will be a place where the undecided and uncommitted will be weeded out.

Your choice of a partner will determine where you will spend eternity!

Part 4:38
What Is a Spiritual Stronghold?

A spiritual stronghold does not just occur by itself. A spiritual stronghold only takes place after the Christian opens the door in his life, making it possible. That explanation brings up a thought that had not occurred to me before. A spiritual stronghold probably is not limited to Christians. Satan wants to create as many of his evil spiritual strongholds as possible in as many humans as he can.

Church pastors have often preached about them, countless books have been written about them, and humans have long fought against them. These are **the works of the flesh** that keep the Christian in bondage to sin. *They are sinful strongholds that Satan has intensified, and they may even have evolved into an addiction in the sinner. In those cases the sinner has been taken over by the demonic realm in that sin.*

Both from the Bible and from other areas, I have compiled a list to review. Each of these listed areas start in the mind and then move into a person's heart or inner being. Once the stronghold moves out of the mind, the thought is put into practice. Once a habit is put into practice, Satan moves into a person, then Satan helps make the thought into an addiction or something harder to break.

The demonic has more than likely been involved in the result long before the habit becomes an addition.

An *addiction* is simply something you cannot get rid of.

Satan helps the work of the flesh begin. He first induces the flesh to desire it and then deserves it or needs it. Once he has you under his control, Satan makes you feel all the negative emotions he can possibly lay on you. In all honesty, when Satan gets a person to that point it is very hard to get free.

In his book, *What Demons Can Do to Saints*, Dr. Merrill F. Unger said that the demons attack the mind to gain a foothold in the life of a person. Satan will blind the minds of the unsaved to keep them from the light of the gospel.

Even in the simple act of bringing the gospel to the unsaved, Satan is involved and tries to hinder the gospel presentation.

Works of the Flesh

Adultery .... *Sexual sin that involves at least one married person*
Fornication .... *Sexual sins involving two unmarried persons*
Homosexuality .... *Sexual sins involving same-sex couples*
Uncleanness .... *Morally unclean; unclean thoughts, foulness, etc.*
Lewdness .... *Anything indecent or offensive in a sexual manner.*
Jealousy .... *Envy, desire*

Part Four: Your Victory Over Satan Begins NOW

Idolatry .... *Anything that takes a position in your life higher than God.*

Hatred .... *Hostility, aversion, enmity, negative feelings, etc.*

Unforgiveness .... Self-explanatory

Contentious .... *Dissension, argumentative*

Wrath .... *Uncontrollable anger*

Selfish Ambitions .... *Desiring something without concern for others*

Heresies .... *Uncontrollable belief in things*

Envy .... *Extreme desire of another's belongings*

Murder .... *Both physical and mental; biblically would include hatred toward another*

Drunkenness .... *Uncontrollable desire of an intoxicant.*

Substance Abuse .... *Overindulgence in or dependence on an addictive substance.*

Revelries .... *Unusual or overindulgence in parties involving other no-no's*

Pornography .... *Anything designed to arouse and/or give sexual pleasure*

I am sure l missed some, but you get the idea of what can be included in the works of the flesh. *A quick review of this list should leave no doubt in your mind exactly how far sinful mankind has fallen from where he was created.* Each of these works of the flesh start in the mind. Allowing the thought to fester in your mind will open the door to the next step of allowing the demonic to slip through.

At the point *the thought* enters your mind, take control and either ask Jesus to remove the thought or take control of the thought and use your authority over the Evil One to order him out. The sinful thought will have been dealt with and is gone.

Should you choose to allow the thought to remain and grow, **Satan will then help you to move the thought out of your mind and into your very being.** Then he will be only too happy to lead you into circumstances where you can indulge your thought into an action. Given enough time, your thought will become an addiction or something you cannot get rid of.

That is the bad news and explains how Satan can take a simple work of the flesh and turn it into something bad or into an addiction. Before you allow the Devil and his helpers to get any work of the flesh into a habit or addiction, know that there is a way out.

Not only is this way out for the Christian, but given God's nature, it will work for anyone. At any point where a person becomes aware of the problem and wants to deal with it, even though it may be hard or having to overcome pride, the solution is simple. A non-Christian only has to cry out in desperation, *"Oh, God, help me!" and He will.* How God will respond to that call of desperation, I don't know, but I do know He will respond.

For a Christian it is easier, but Satan will use all his tricks, lies, and deceit to forestall your cry to God for help.

Satan will attempt to lie to you by telling you that you are too far gone for God to help you. He will send the spirit of doubt into your mind, and that spirit will tell you anything to keep you from believing that a loving God wants to help you.

Before I share how a Christian must make a request from God for His help and ultimate solution, I want to review the players and what they have to offer.

Part 4:39
Which God/god Would You Choose?

- Satan is the fallen god.
- Satan is a liar.
- Satan is a deceiver.
- Satan is a thief.
- Satan is a murderer.
- Satan is a god of fear.
- Satan is a god of doubt.
- Satan will cause your mind to question heaven.
- Satan is the god of depression.
- Satan will tell you that you are not worthy of heaven.

God Is the God Who is Directly Opposite

- God is the God of love.
- God never lies.
- God never deceives.
- God was willing to sacrifice His Son for you.
- God has an eternal heavenly place for you.
- God can and will remove your fear.
- God can and will remove your doubts.
- God, through Jesus, will forgive ALL your sins.
- God, through Jesus, has deliverance from the Enemy, healing for sickness, and health for your body.

When you compare the two offerings, the choice would appear to be a no-brainer.

However, consider the following:
- A Christian can know the truth intellectually, but that knowledge does not mean he will live his life like he really believes.
- God makes all on the list available, but one more should be on the list.
  - **God will also give you faith to believe His promises.**
- You need to know what He promises you. The only way you will know what those promises are is to read and study your Bible.
  - **All of what you are reading in this book is yours for the asking.**

I promised to share how a Christian can handle a sinful fleshly problem in the early stages or even when Satan has taken control. When your flesh allows a temptation to enter your mind, order it out in Jesus' name, and it will go. At this stage, the temptation is not a sin.

The longer you allow the temptation to linger in your mind, the harder it will be to get rid of it. When allowed to linger **the temptation** becomes a sin. However, when the Holy Spirit makes you aware of what you are allowing to linger in your mind, you can **command** the thought or thoughts to get out in Jesus' name, and they will go. Then you simply ask God to forgive you. Jesus will supply the power that guarantees the sin is gone.

If you ignore the prompting of the Holy Spirit to act on the thought, or thoughts, the door is then opened far enough for a demonic spirit to sneak in, and he will.

Another issue to address is the matter of a **secret sin**, one that you think only you knows about. Secret sins are like termites in a house.

No one knows that they are present until the damage is done. Then it is too late for an easy fix. **A *secret sin* is one that Satan will try to convince you hurts no one simply because you think no one knows about it.**

First, God knows about it, and if you say you are a Christian, He will not let you get away with the sin.

God will expose you unless you have already abandoned Him.

God will either help you get rid of the "termites" or allow you to move to a realm where termites are acceptable.

Funny thing about Satan…after he has gotten you to the place he wants you, he will see that your secret sin is revealed. Unless you are willing to confess and get rid of this secret sin in your life, do not expect deliverance or healing from God.

Part 4:40
Repentance Is Not an Emotion: It Is a Choice

I will not **pray directly** for the person who asks me to pray for their deliverance or their healing. **What I will do is pray with people and lead them in how to lead themselves into deliverance or healing.** Others more mature in these deliverances and healing fields will know how to pray in the knowledge of the Holy Spirit, and they can do so.

Dealing with Satan and his demonic realm is not a game; rather, it is a deadly encounter that involves you and the Devil, who knows the perimeters of all the rules God has determined he must operate within. You and I are most likely not even aware of the boundaries God has placed on the Enemy.

Trust me, if you do not know the rules of what you are involved in, it will be very hard to win. Even wars have rules, and we are at war with a very large, very sophisticated, very unprincipled, very intelligent, and a very evil opponent.

In the apostle John's first letter, he clearly stated that you through Jesus Christ would overcome the evil of the Enemy. That assistance includes the desires of the flesh, the evil Enemy, and all his host.

I want to return to *how Satan operates in a person, including a Christian's life*. At this point, your thought or thoughts will transition into an actuality. The lustful thoughts, for example, will suddenly find an opportunity for a physical relationship. The opportunities for a party with many choices to drink or indulge in other activities will seem to come out of nowhere. A hateful thought for someone will be reinforced, making the hate even more vengeful.

If you pray, admit the sin, and ask God to forgive you, He will always do so. But you may need some help in either praying the prayer or asking for help to take authority over Satan to overcome the problem. Go to your pastor or another Christian you trust. Explain your problem and ask the person to pray with you or to help you take your deliverance from Satan. *Don't wait!*

Once again, the decision comes down to being your choice!

Part 4:41
Satan's Boundaries

God will not allow Satan to do some things. Even in heaven Satan had boundaries that he was not allowed to circumvent.

- **Satan cannot drive God out of your life. Only you can decide you no longer want God in your life. You can decide that you want to enjoy the short-term benefits of a sin more than God.**
  - **Sexual sins come immediately to mind.**

- The love of money is another sin that can overwhelm a person.
- Obsession with power is more common than many Christians believe.
- Addiction to a substance is one that only God can help a Christian overcome totally.

These are examples of only a few of the sins that can entice a person to no longer want God in his life.

Satan cannot cause you to sin. He can lead you into the temptation. He can and will lie to you about how much you need something that you know is sin.

And, after all, God is a God of love, and He would want you to have that which you desire, wouldn't He?

But you and you alone make the decision to sin.

Satan cannot penetrate the shield of your faith *unless you choose to let in the doubts and fear*, which are from the Enemy.

God has promised you protection from doubts and fears, and He has told you to deal with those thoughts immediately when they enter your mind. This book has shared how and when to handle those thoughts.

Satan cannot rob you of your standing as a child of God. **However, he can keep your relationship to God from being the relationship God has promised you.** You can let the Devil steal that closer walk with God you desire by believing his lies, his deceptions, his deceit, or by following his temptations. **Or you can choose to use your God-given authority and order him out of your mind, and therefore, out of your life.**

In John 10, Jesus made very clear what Satan wants to do to man.

This passage has already been addressed, *but keep in mind these words came directly from Jesus.* There is no question that Satan is a liar. And unless you want to call Jesus (and indirectly God) a liar, **then believe the words Jesus spoke.**

Jesus was not willing to let His warning about Satan's intentions end there. Jesus went on in verse 10 to tell us why He came to earth. After reading the verse, **stop, think, and then shout, "Hallelujah! Praise the Lord."**

Part 4:42
Demonic Affiliations

What am I talking about? Frankly, very few people, including Christians, know that these affiliations are from the Devil. Involvement in any of these demonic organizations or involvement of what you may think are harmless games will allow the Enemy a right to move into your life.

First on the list is water divination or *dowsing* or *water witching*. A simple explanation of this ability is when a person takes a forked stick, holds the forked end, and walks around until the single end vibrates and turns down, indicating the presence of water.

As a very young teen growing up on the farm, my parents needed to drill a well to water the crops. *We hired a person who specialized in this dousing practice. We watched him walk around until the stick turned downward. Sure enough, a well was drilled there, and we found water.*

Having that ability looked like fun to my brother and my cousin, so for a long time we all ran around with a forked stick. Years later when I read a book entitled, *Angels of Light: False Prophets and Deceiv-*

Part Four: Your Victory Over Satan Begins NOW

ing Spirits at Work Today in the Church and World. The author, Eddie Hyatt, mentioned that playing around with **water divination** opens the door to an uncontrollable obsession with pornographic material. This had been a problem I could not get rid of—no matter how much I prayed. I found someone who could lead me in a prayer of deliverance, and that obsession was broken.

I say all this to point out that I did not know what I was fooling around with was a sin. And second, ***even in my innocence, Satan moved in.***

With that said, I will list several institutions, groups, games, readings, etc. for those who have opened a door in your life for the enemy to move in. If you identify with any of the listed subjects and if you have a sin, a harassment, a problem with dead prayers, falling asleep in church, and no interest in things of God, go online or purchase a book on the involvement to see if that may be the answer.

Ask God to reveal to you what is hindering you in the things of God. Trust me, the Holy Spirit will bring the answer, likely in a way or manner you never considered. Please note the following demonic affiliations:

- Cults
- False Religions
- Black magic
- Witchcraft
- Soothsaying
- Séances
- Water Divination
- Channeling *(trying to contact the dead)*
- The Occult
- Sorcery of any kind
- Open sexual activity
- Abortion
- Tarot Cards
- Waning
- Horoscopes

This list is certainly not comprehensive, and if you are aware of one not listed, check the Internet to see if that could be a problem in your life.

I am not addressing these in detail; for you to check out those that may be hindering your relationship to God is better. Keep in mind that what He has promised you is yours. If you have been involved in any of these affiliations, and you have a problem that will not go away, become knowledgeable about the subject biblically. Confess your sin of involvement to God and ask forgiveness, then use your authority to command that demonic entity to depart from you in Jesus' name.

Thank Jesus for your freedom and give God the praise He deserves. It doesn't matter if you found the Lord after your involvement in any of these; they will not simply go away. You allowed the Enemy in, and until you order him out in Jesus' name, he will stay and continue to trouble you.

Part 4:43
Demonic Spirits or Demons Found in the Bible

Demon of Leprosy .... Luke 5:13

Demon of Arthritis .... Luke 13:11
(Much arthritis is not age-related and is exacerbated.)

Demon of Death .... Hebrews 2:14

Spirit of Religion *(blinds eyes to the truth)* .... Colossians 2:20-21

Spirit of Foolishness .... Isaiah 19:12-14; I Corinthians 2:14
(The Word sounds even more foolish to man.)

Spirit of Jealousy .... Numbers 5:14-30

Spirit of Muteness *(or speech)* .... Mark 9:32-33

Spirit of Infirmity .... Luke 13:18
(A spirit of sickness can exacerbate a sickness like cancer.)

Part Four: Your Victory Over Satan Begins NOW

Spirit of Divination *(Fortune-telling)* .... Acts 16:16

Spirit that Distresses............................. 1 Samuel 16:14

Unclean Spirits................................. Matthew 12:13

Spirit of Rebellion .... 1 Samuel 15:23

Spirit of Violence..................... Psalm 11:5, Proverbs 3:31

Spirit of Abuse ....1 Peter 4:3, Colossians 3:8

Spirit of Pride *(one of the worst for a Christian)* ..Proverbs 8:13, 16:5

Spirit of Suicide .... I Corinthians 10:13
(Allied with the demon of death, a Christian can commit suicide.)

Spirit of Abortion ....Psalm 139:13-16; Exodus 20:13

Spirit of Depression..................... Isaiah 41:10, Psalm 34:8

Spirit of Fever *(Peter's mother-in-law healed)*.......... Luke 4:38-40

Spirit of Addiction *(can't quit something)*....... 1 Corinthians 10:13

Spirit of Lust............. Matthew 5:27-29, 1 Corinthians 6:18-19
(Difficult to overcome, this spirit can be physical or pornographic.)

Spirit of Demonic Activities .... Ephesians 6:10-11, James 4:7

Spirit of Error ....John 8:32, Ephesians 4:14
(Why some people cannot admit to being wrong)

A Hindering Spirit......................... 2 Corinthians 4:3-4
(Keeps us from reading the Bible or understanding it)

Spirit of Mind Hindrance.................... 2 Corinthians 4:3-4
(Blockage of understanding with your mind)

Spirit of Bondage................................ Romans 8:15

Spirit of Disobedience *(refusal to obey)* .... Ephesians 2:2

Spirit of Fear *(why some Christians live in fear)*. ...... 2 Timothy 1:7

Spirit of Antichrist .... 1 John 4
   (Believes in anything that belittles or denies Christ)

On a more positive note, one spirit is known as the **Spirit of Truth**. Many more Bible passages can be found to address the various spirits listed by using a search engine like Google.

If you even think a demonic spirit is involved in your life, take the authority that Jesus made available to the Christian, and use that authority to rebuke the demon; command him to leave in the power of Jesus' name. Then ask the Holy Spirit to fill the void left by the demonic spirit's departure.

For the most part, the church, denominational beliefs, and religious theology have conformed to cultural beliefs over the years rather than biblical truth. Satan has been very helpful in helping various theologians come to these conclusions. *And with all the prestigious "letters" behind their name, it is only reasonable for insignificant religious mortals to believe they are correct, rather than search the Scriptures for the truth!* The Bible says that Satan can appear as an angel of light, and one way is through so-called learned theologians.

John also made an interesting observation in I John 4:1 (ESV): *"Beloved, do not believe every spirit, but test the spirits to see whether they are from God, for many false prophets have gone out into the world."*

Prophets in that day would be the equivalent of preachers, teachers, and theologians of today.

Paul stated the issue a bit differently in 2 Corinthians 11 when he said the following:

Part Four: Your Victory Over Satan Begins NOW

"God never sent these men at all; they are 'phonies' who have fooled you into thinking they are Christ's apostles. [14]Yet I am not surprised! Satan can change himself into an angel of light, [15]so it is no wonder his servants can do it too, and seem like godly ministers..." (vv. 13-15 TLB).

Even today Satan has ministers who appear to be genuine ministers of the gospel, but in reality, they are really agents for Satan. Sometimes they will not even be aware that they are being used by Satan.

Sadly, some ministers see the ministry as an easy way to make a living. Some ministers, even those with an abundance of letters behind their name, have been fooled by Satan and are teaching so-called truths not found in the Bible.

The only way for the average saint not be taken in by false preachers and teachers is to know the Word for himself! *However, in today's churches, sermons, Bible classes, Sunday school classes, etc., the leaders are taking the easy way out and showing videos rather than teaching from the Word.* Now don't get me wrong most of these videos are fine, but they only present another man's opinion who the listeners do not know.

In the fifth chapter of Peter's first letter, the apostle reminds us that our fight against the Enemy is not a one-time matter; rather, it is a constant and probably daily battle.

When Jesus had the experience of dealing with the Devil in the wilderness, the last word in one translation clearly stated that Satan only left Jesus until a more opportune time arose. Take my word for it, that Satan's departure for a later apropos time is also a very true statement for every Christian. Peter reminds us that in the fight against the Enemy we must be sober and vigilant.

We must be vigilant about what we hear and read; we could be taken in. The only way to avoid being seduced by wrong doctrine is to study and know the Word of God.

Part 4:44
Strongholds Caused by Negative Emotions

A *stronghold* is an area invaded by Satan or one of his demons that has taken control in your life. Try as you may, you cannot get rid of it. A *demonic stronghold* or a *negative emotion* is usually caused by an action that you have not addressed. And because you did not deal with that emotion, it is now an area that Satan has taken control of within you. Some of these areas of negative emotions, or feelings include the following:

- Bitterness
- Hatred
- Depression
- Obsessive fear
- Addiction
- Same-sex relationships
- Perfectionism
- Selfishness
- A Lack of forgiveness
- Shame
- Obsessive worry
- Jealousy
- Lust
- Adultery
- Control
- Fragile ego

Satan can take advantage of a situation where, under ordinary circumstances, you would not allow him in. *This can happen when an experience like an unexpected or untimely death occurs, a spirit of depression moves in, and you cannot rise above the level of depression.*

> *Perhaps you struggle with money, which causes undue worry, and Satan moves in.*

Part Four: Your Victory Over Satan Begins NOW

> *Perhaps you want what your neighbor has, and you become jealous.*

> *Perhaps you want to control others, including your family.*

> *Perhaps you are attracted to another person of the same gender.*

> **Perhaps someone treats you wrong, and you cannot forgive.**

> *You or a loved one suffers from a sickness or disease, and your normal defenses are down.*

The list is endless, and the bottom line is that the Enemy has moved into an area of your life. **The sad part is that the Enemy will attempt to justify your negative emotions.** Satan will not let you deal with these emotions on your own; he or his angels will keep you dealing with these emotions for as long as possible.

The Holy Spirit is the One Who will help you overcome them. Ask for His help and guidance. Your pastor or another Christian can walk you through how to deal with them. But again, you will need to make the decision that you want out of the situation in which you find yourself. Then go directly to God and ask for His Holy Spirit to guide you in what to do. **Then do it!**

This teaching book on *Father God, the Devil and You* is quickly coming to a conclusion; therefore, a little review can't hurt. **Satan does NOT have the right to rule or dominate the Christian.**

In the information quest leading to the penning of this book, it became evident the average believer in Christ has more faith in Satan's authority and power than he has in God's power and authority. Proof of that statement can be found in Colossians 1:12-13.

The tactics of the Enemy were addressed, and I have listed six of the most prominent ones:

1) Failing to forgive
2) Bitterness
3) Rejection
4) Addiction
5) Fear
6) Pride

There is no question that the saints of the church are at war with the Devil and his hosts of fallen angels.

When you realize a problem or when the Holy Spirit brings a situation to the forefront of your mind, use your authority to command that evil entity to get out in Jesus' powerful name; then ask God for forgiveness. Don't let your pride keep you from seeking and asking for forgiveness. Father God is just waiting. **Keep in mind that repentance is not an emotion, but a choice.**

The entire book in one way or another is related to faith. Talking about faith is easy but living by faith is something else entirely. Simply put, **faith to live by is saying that faith is when we believe that Jesus is Who He says He is and will do what He promises to do.**

Over the years I have learned that the more I learned about the Devil, the more God has required of me. And the more you know about the Devil, the more he will attack you *and your entire family*. But the more I learned, **the more I learned to trust God.** The more I learned to trust, the more *fun* I had joining with Father God and His Son in defeating the Enemy.

I trust that God will let me keep on learning about the Enemy and my authority over him through Jesus Christ. The battle has been interesting, and I have not always won initially. But I have won in the end.

The apostle Peter said it so well: *"One will only defeat the devil when you get a foundation of God's Word, and then you act on it"* (1 Peter 5:9 TLB).

PART FIVE

Father God, the Devil, and You

Conclusion, Summary, and Challenge

Conclusion, Summary, and Challenge

As this book is coming to its end, my hope is that you will continue on in the study of the Word as it relates to this subject.

The book began with a look at Satan, where he came from, how he related in God's spiritual realm, his rebellion against God, where he is now, his future rule in his domain first on earth, and then his banishment to hell for eternity.

The second part of the book dealt with your authority in Christ Jesus over the Enemy currently here on this earth. **As a Christian with Jesus as your Savior, you reign in heaven with Him now.**

In addition, you are responsible for carrying out the work of Jesus against the Devil while you are on earth. Jesus said that He came to defeat the works of the Devil. Jesus came, died, rose, and ascended to heaven. The Devil had been defeated, and when Jesus ascended into heaven, the Devil was kicked out.

Jesus is no longer on earth defeating the Devil. Now the work of defeating the Devil daily is the responsibility of the church, Christ's body.

The third part covered spiritual warfare and the believers' involvement in this spiritual warfare. Dr. Tom Sexton stated in his manual, *Bringing Men to Christ*, that all Scriptures taken as a whole are true. That fact being stated, it would follow that what is found in the Scriptures in their entirety could be summed up in the following statements:

Part Five: Conclusion, Summary, and Challenge

- It takes the same faith from the Holy Spirit to believe for the forgiveness of your sins as it does for believing for deliverance from Satan's attacks and for other promises in the Bible.

- It takes the same commitment to Jesus Christ to live for Him after you have invited Him into your life as it does to trust Him in other areas of your daily living.

- It takes the same reading of the Bible to understand your promise for eternal life as it does to understand and believe that Jesus' defeat of the Devil is also your promise to defeat him daily.

- It takes the same prayers to God thanking Him for your eternal life and the forgiveness of your sins as it does for thanking Him for sending Jesus to deliver you from Satan and to heal you from sickness.

- It takes the same faith that there is a God Who created the universe.

- It takes the same faith to believe that Jesus was sent to pay the penalty for your sins as it does to believe that Jesus made it possible for you to defeat Satan in His name in with His power.

- It takes the same faith in the work of the Holy Spirit to give you faith to believe Jesus died to pay the price for your sins as it does for you to have faith that Jesus can deliver you from the realm of Satan and to heal you from your sicknesses.

Satan can attack any one of these areas individually, so be aware and take action as needed.

Note: Lifting up God's Word does not mean picking it up so you can dust beneath it.

- You will not defeat Satan if you do not know the Word.
- You will not be healed unless you know the Word.
- You will not know the promises found in the Bible unless you read and know the Word.
- You will not recognize or defeat temptation unless you know the Word.
- You will not know the Holy Spirit is waiting to watch over you unless you know the Word. **If you want victory through Jesus over the Devil,** *stay in the Word.* **If you want victory over sickness through Jesus,** *stay in the Word.* **If you want the assurance of your salvation for eternal life,** *stay in the Word.*

  The apostle Paul said it so well in Romans 10:17 (NKJV) when he said: *"So then faith comes by hearing, and hearing by the word of God."*

The following are a few verses from Dr. Tom Sexton's work that plainly show why you need to spend time in the Bible.

- In Romans 1:16 (NKJV) Paul wrote, *"For I am not ashamed of the gospel of Christ, for it is the power of God...."*
  - Everything in this book starts with the premise that I'm not ashamed of the gospel found in the Bible.
- In Psalm 107:20 (NKJV) the Psalmist wrote these words well before the time of Jesus on this earth. *"He sent His word and healed them, and delivered them from their destructions."*

Part Five: Conclusion, Summary, and Challenge

- This book is on your authority over the Enemy. Paul wrote the following in 2 Corinthians 10:4 (NKJV): *"For the weapons of our warfare are not carnal, but mighty in God for pulling down strongholds."*

- In Matthew 16:18b (NKJV), Jesus made it very clear what the strongholds really are when He said the following: *"I will build My church, and the gates of Hades [Hell] shall not prevail against it."*

  - Satan loses, and the church of Jesus Christ wins.

- Over the years I have encountered numerous Christians who were not assured of their salvation. This book has addressed how the lack of assurance is a favorite tactic of the Enemy.

  - I John 5:13 (NKJV) addresses that issue: *"These things I have written to you who believe in the name of the Son of God, that you may know that you have eternal life, and that you may continue to believe in the name of the Son of God."*

- Paul knew that the Devil would make the assurance of your salvation a key target when he wrote in 2 Corinthians 4:4 (NKJV): *"whose minds the god of this age has blinded, who do not believe, lest the light of the gospel of the glory of Christ, who is the image of God, should shine on them."*

  - The same Devil who keeps men from believing in Jesus Christ puts doubts of your salvation in your mind.

The gospel of Jesus Christ is a glorious gospel because it is trustworthy. The Holy Spirit gave you your faith to believe for your salvation; don't let the Devil cause you to doubt. Use your authority over him in Jesus' name and command that demon of doubt to leave. *Try it; feeling the demon leave brings pleasure.*

The Holy Spirit gave you the faith for your salvation. He does not stop there. He will also remove any spirit of doubt the Enemy throws at you.

Your part is the command for him to leave, and then Jesus backs up your command with His power.

It is time to join with Jesus in His victory over Satan and his kingdom.

Heaven or Hell –
Victory or Failure

I would be remiss if I ended his book without reminding you again that heaven or hell is your choice.

The choice for heaven is one that you and you alone must make. The choice for hell has already been made for you when Adam sinned.

By default, *or by doing nothing,* you have made your choice FOR HELL, and Satan will do all in his power to keep you from choosing heaven.

You may think you are not as bad as some others you know, but that excuse will not qualify you for heaven.

You have sinned. A little or a lot doesn't matter; *you have sinned.* A seriously bad sin or just a little lie doesn't matter; *you have sinned.*

You may think you have a lot of time left to make that decision, and *you might be right. However, death also comes as a thief in the night.* Father God does not send you a notice warning you that it is your time to die.

If you put off your decision to invite Jesus into your life, then you

Part Five: Conclusion, Summary, and Challenge

are saying you really would like to spend eternity in hell with Satan. But a simple prayer can move you from eternity in hell with Satan; to Heaven with Jesus.

Pray this simple prayer from your heart:

Father God, I want to accept this free gift of eternal life. Please forgive me of all the sins that I have committed.

Please forgive me for not loving You as I should have. Thank You for sending Jesus to die for me and for providing His blood to place a barrier so that You no longer see my sins.

Jesus, would You take control of the rest of my life?

And I ask You to send the Holy Spirit into my life to provide the assurance of spending eternity in Your beautiful heaven.

Father God, thank You for hearing and answering this prayer that I have prayed from my heart.

Your eternal life in heaven starts now. You are right now seated with Jesus in heaven. You right now have the authority over the Devil and his fallen angels.

Every victory you have read in this book is now yours. Claim them and use them because Jesus paid a terrific price so that you could.

Reference Works

Neil T. Anderson and Timothy M. Warner. *The Beginner's Guide to Spiritual Warfare*. Bloomington, Minn.: Bethany House Publishers, 2008.

Heiser, Michael S. *Demons: What the Bible Really Says About the Powers of Darkness*. Bellingham, Wash.: Lexham Press, 2020.

_____. *The Unseen Realm: Recovering the Supernatural Worldview of the Bible*. Bellingham, Wash.: Lexham Press, 2019.

Hagin, Kenneth E. *The Believer's Authority*. Tulsa: Kenneth Hagin Ministries, 1985.

Kraft, Charles H. T*he Rules of Engagement: Understanding the Principles that Govern the Spiritual Battles in Our Lives*. Eugene, Ore.: Wipf and Stock, 2005.

Murphy, Dr. Ed. *The Handbook for Spiritual Warfare*. Nashville: Thomas Nelson, 2003.

Pierce, Chuck D. *The Spiritual Warfare Handbook: How to Battle, Pray and Prepare Your House for Triumph*. Ada, Mich.: Chosen Books, 2016.

Many additional works can be found by checking the Internet.

Bible Translations

Scriptures noted TLB are taken from The Living Bible, copyright © 1971 by Tyndale House Foundation. Used by permission of Tyndale House Publishers Inc., Carol Stream, Illinois 60188. All rights reserved.

Scriptures noted KJV are taken from the King James Bible, public domain.

Scriptures noted NIV are taken from the Holy Bible, New International Version®, NIV® Copyright ©1973, 1978, 1984, 2011 by Biblica, Inc.® Used by permission. All rights reserved worldwide.

Scriptures noted NKJV are taken from the Holy Bible, the New King James Version®. Copyright © 1982 by Thomas Nelson. Used by permission. All rights reserved.

Scriptures noted AKJV are taken from the Holy Bible, the Authorized (King James) Version (AKJV). KJV reproduced by permission of Cambridge University Press, the Crown's patentee in the UK.

Scriptures noted NKJV are taken from the Holy Bible, English Standard Version. ESV® Text Edition: 2016. Copyright © 2001 by Crossway Bibles, a publishing ministry of Good News Publishers.

Scriptures noted NLT are taken from the Holy Bible, New Living Translation, copyright © 1996, 2004, 2015 by Tyndale House Foundation. Used by permission of Tyndale House Publishers, Inc., Carol Stream, Illinois 60188. All rights reserved.

Scriptures noted RSV are taken from the Revised Standard Version of the Bible, copyright © 1946, 1952, and 1971 the Division of Christian Education of the National Council of the Churches of Christ in the United States of America. Used by permission. All rights reserved.